"If you love the English language, reading, writing, speaking, storytelling, history, and quirky humor, you'll love this book."
> –Craig Wiesner, Reach and Teach bookstore

"Ms. Hammer brings punctuation to life."
> –Greg Keech, Chair, Department of English as a Second Language, City College of San Francisco

uendet alteri : quātocūqz fuerit āte eſti=
matū. Omne qđ đūo cōſecrat ſiue ho=
mo fuerit ſiue animal·ſiue ager non
ueniet:nec redimi poterit quicquid ſe=
mel fuerit cōſecratū. Sanctū ſanctorū
erit đūo. Et ois cōſecratio q̄ offert ab
hoīe nō redimetur:ſed morte mori=
etur. Omnes decime tre ſiue đe pomis

Johannes Gutenberg, approximately 1455,
with early examples of punctuation.

Albert Drosoph's
Field Guide to Punctuation

*For the Observant, the Dismissive,
the Curious, the Confused*

By Jenny Hammer

GRIZZLY PEAK PRESS
350 Berkeley Park Blvd. Kensington, CA 94707

For information contact:

Grizzly Peak Press
350 Berkeley Park Boulevard
Kensington, CA 94707
grizzlypeakpress.com

Albert Drosoph's Field Guide to Punctuation
is published by Daniel N. David
and is distributed by Grizzly Peak Press.

Used with permission:
"For you have learned, not what to say, /
But how the saying must be said."
~ J. V. Cunningham

Design, layout and typesetting by
Sara B. Brownell • sarabbrownell.com

ISBN Number: 978-0-9988310-0-8
Library of Congress Number: 2017936869

Printed in the United States of America

For my mother,
Marion Bowers Hammer,
whose creative nature inspired my own

Table of Contents

Preface

Some time ago, a young girl named Arden Evers visited my place of business and was surprised to learn that punctuation marks could be raised in captivity. She was evidently quite bright yet did not seem to know very much about what punctuation is and can do.

It occurred to me a few weeks after her visit that I perhaps needed to help her and others like her improve their writing and reading by advertising my products and giving a little instruction about their use. Punctuation marks are not unnecessary or dull. They serve to make meanings clear, and clarity in communication is important. Clarity prevents misunderstandings.

Though I am a businessman, I would be less than honest if I said that you had to—or even should—purchase punctuation from me. You can find punctuation marks in the wild if you know how and where to look and what to look for. Punctuation marks are visible to the unaided eye. In addition, the natural resource of punctuation is in the public domain—like so many good and important things—so I need to point out this fact: The marks are found everywhere, and all are free to find and use them. Their purchase from my vivarium is unnecessary.

Rather than as an advertisement of my services, I have written this field guide to assist in the identification and understanding of these marks. For writers, its purpose is to encourage "proper" (expected) usage, so there is ease and clarity in the communication of your ideas to readers. The effective use of punctuation by writers helps readers read better.

For readers, its purpose is to help you decipher meaning in what you read, so you will understand what writers who adhere to this compact of clarity communicate.

I feel sure that, once you can identify, use, and understand the many marks in the world, you will realize the power that punctuation affords you and will employ these marks to good effect.

Happy reading and happy writing!

Introduction

I have arranged this field guide alphabetically by common (lay) terms. The Latin taxonomy is included only for clarity and for more definitive identification. This Latin nomenclature can also help you see the relationships of purpose among the different marks by family, genus, and species. I intentionally did not order the punctuation marks by frequency of use or by Linnaeus's classification because I felt an alphabetical-by-lay-terms order would be best for the user in finding, identifying, or using a punctuation mark quickly and easily.

As to the example sentences, I have turned my attention to the natural world, the importance of which was impressed upon me by the very same young girl who inspired me to assemble this field guide in the first place. Arden Evers's description of the world outside my vivarium door made me realize that punctuation is not all that's important, though important it is. One must go out and observe the natural world, for in that is cause for amazement and understanding.

Few human inventions can compare with the complexity of life in its myriad forms or even the complexity of the inanimate on earth or beyond. Study of the natural world will always surprise us and exercise our innate capabilities of celebration. The real world is here; we need only pay attention to it. By ignoring the naturally-given bounty and beauty of reality, we risk losing it.

As a consequence of Arden's visit, I plunged into researching and observing these very real things that I had previously viewed as inconsequential. I used some of what I learned thereby in my examples for each species of punctuation. It took the stories and experience of a 10-year-old girl to jar me out of the parochialism of my pristine vivarium and to focus my attention on the what of communication instead of merely the how.

There may be some who will accuse me of being a prescriptivist. However, if clarity is the goal, certain expectations and conventions are necessary; if we lose clarity, we do no one any favors. This field guide attempts to describe the way these many marks are conventionally used by writers and to describe to others where these marks can be and what these marks are doing. By describing the marks and their habitat, I am hardly giving a linguistic prescription.

Don't be lulled, however, into thinking change is not necessary. As you will see from the historical records of these marks, change is the norm. If something is wrong or doesn't work—no matter how long its tradition or how sacrosanct it has become—changing it is not only necessary, it is our duty.

But change for the sake of change only, or change for the wrong reasons, is also a mistake. The usage of punctuation and the marks themselves have evolved but the underlying need—clear communication—has not changed. What has become conventional has become so because it works and because it has benefitted us. Ease of understanding another's thoughts and ease of communicating one's own thoughts to others through the written word is a crucial reason for punctuation in the first place.

I am not a grammarian. You will not read in this field guide terms like nominative, accusative, interrogative, genitive, subjective, objective, attributive, predicative, or possessive. My focus is on punctuation. In consequence, to the greatest extent possible, I will not use many of the traditional terms of grammar. Some readers will find this a relief; others will chastise me for being "lite."

However, the modern English language has for too long been shoehorned into the grammar of Latin, a position from which it has often pushed readers and students into the throes of despair. It is my feeling that antiquated grammatical terms cloud common understanding of the language and prevent important discussions and descriptions of it.

What is important is not the name of something, but, rather, where it came from (ancestral record/pedigree); what it looks like (description/field marks); its purpose; how it behaves and what it does (voice); and where a person can find it (range/habitat). This is as true of the marks of punctuation as it is for people; you will know them as they do. I have, however, included a glossary for some of the terms I must use.

Of course, it makes no sense to attempt to communicate when the would-be communicator is bereft of ideas. It is important for writers to actually have something to say. No amount of clarifying punctuation can overcome improperly substantiated ideas.

A thought needs to be tested with discussion and debate and counter-argument in order to emerge and soar as "true." Opinions require support. I sincerely hope not to foster a sad outcome such as described in a poem by J.V. Cunningham: "For you have learned, not what to say, / But how the saying must be said."

Good punctuation makes clear—and highlights—the connections and relatedness of ideas. Without it, writing is a jumble, a chaos, setting readers up for fitful starts, re-readings, and the making of erroneous guesses about how ideas fit or relate. If punctuation is good, it is proper. If it is good, it is correct. If it is correct, it connects . . . on many levels.

Our linguistic evolution from grunts and cries to poetry is one of the singular achievements of humankind. The complexity of language has formed us human just as the complexity of life has formed the world. Yet many of us have become thrilled, quite understandably, by our other devices so much we ignore the intricacies and importance of what, at its very heart, sustains us.

Go out into that tangible world. Go to the world of the written word. Look very carefully at where you are and all that is there. Observe. Use these punctuation tools of clarity and connection to share all that you find and come to understand there. If there is a goal for this field guide, connections and clarity are it.

A Note About "Exotics"

Originally, I was not going to include examples of "exotics"—punctuation found where it never traditionally was. However, since there is a high probability you will come across specimens of Narratopsida Scriberales Interpunctidae outside their native habitats, I feel it is important to point out these occurrences.

Like rats jumping ships onto isolated islands, zebra clams spreading from the discharged ballast water of ships, water hyacinths introduced as ornamentals and then clogging lakes, or French broom annihilating native vegetation once it escapes from backyard landscaping, punctuation has become an exotic and invasive species, as well, threatening clear writing.

Consequently, in this guide, I will sometimes point out where you might find punctuation marks "as exotics," in locations where they should not be. I have added examples, so—should you come across marks in these places—you can take steps, as I do, to re-balance the natural order of things. Please catch the errant marks and move them back to the habitats in which they belong. In this way, they can thrive and do the work they evolved to do—providing clarity for both readers and writers.

Albert F. Drosoph

Albert Drosoph's
Field Guide to Punctuation

For the Observant, the Dismissive,
the Curious, the Confused

Abbreviations

CLASS:	Narratopsida
ORDER:	Scriberales
FAMILY:	Breviaridae
GENUS:	*Tenerampalis*
SPECIES:	*T. exigumspatium*

Description/ Field Marks:	**Abbreviations are shortenings of words.** Letters of the word are discarded and the remaining letters usually end with a period. Most of the time, an abbreviation is comprised of the first letters of a word. Sometimes, however, the abbreviation is cobbled together from non-sequential letters. Abbreviations usually should not be used in formal writing.
Voice:	Writers use abbreviations when there isn't enough room to write out the whole word, when they are too lazy to do so, or when the abbreviation is very common (Mr., Ms., Dr., St.)
Range/Habitat:	Abbreviations are often found on envelopes and other mailings, in notations for personal use, and on forms.
Examples:	*She was born on Nov. 26, 2002.* (November)
	She was born on 26 Nov. 2002. (November)
	Dr. Loon was a very demanding researcher. (Doctor)

Not True North St. is in the town of Ankh. (Street)

Gen. Malaise had been pursuing her for many days. (General)

I have sent many dinra signs to Del Rey, Inc. over the years. (Incorporated)

Comments: Be careful, as some abbreviations look the same but have different meanings. You will need to use context to decide what word they are an abbreviation of.

Dr. (Doctor)

Dr. (Drive, for an address)

St. (Street, for an address)

St. (Saint, in front of a name)

In addition, not all abbreviations are shortened to the first few letters.

Blvd. (Boulevard, for an address)

Mt. or *Mtn.* (Mountain or Mount)

Some common abbreviations are the shortening of Latin words:

v. or *vs.* (*versus*, "opposing")

etc. (*et cetera*, "and so forth," "at the end of a list")

et al. (*et alia*, "and others")

i.e. (*id est*, "that is," "in other words")

e.g. (*exempli gratia*, "for example")

Some abbreviations require a period.

Ph.D. (Doctor of Philosophy)

Mrs.

Ms.

Mr.

Jr. (Junior, after a name)

a.m. (in the morning)

p.m. (in the afternoon)

B.C. (before Christ, used after a date)

A.D. (*Anno Domini*, used before a date)

A.H. (*anno Hegirae*, used after a date)

B.C.E. (before the common era, used after a date)

C.E. (common era, used after a date)

Other abbreviations do not require a period.

V (volts)

DC (direct current)

C (Celsius, a measurement of temperature)

Hz (Hertz, a measurement of frequency)

kg (kilograms)

g (grams)

m (meters)

cm (centimeters)

mm (millimeters)

rpm (revolutions per minute)

h or hr (hour)

mph (miles per hour)

km (kilometers)

km/h (kilometers per hour)

ghg (greenhouse gas(es))

Some are written with or without periods.

CEO or C.E.O. (Chief Executive Officer)

E.R. or ER (Emergency Room)

I.C.U. or ICU (Intensive Care Unit)

Perhaps you have heard recordings of the eerie songs of whales. The earth itself also sings though the radio frequencies of these songs are too low or high for us to hear. Human speech is in the 80-1600 Hz range. Whales emit sounds in the 10-52 Hz range. The radio frequencies of earth are in the 7.83-11,000 Hz range.

Many forms of measurement are abbreviated when they are used in technical writing and with numbers.

At sea level, water boils at 100° C.

Oak tree height: 20 m.

Let the tank dry for 4 hrs. prior to using.

A spider silk long enough to circle the earth would weigh less than 500 kg.

Light travels at the speed of 299,792.458 km/sec.

Acronyms

CLASS:	Narratopsida
ORDER:	Scriberales
FAMILY:	Breviaridae
GENUS:	*Tenvis*
SPECIES:	*T. locus*

Description/ Field Marks:	**Acronyms are abbreviations that are spoken as words or letters.** They consist of the initial letter of each word, written as a capital letter. You will most often see acronyms without periods between their initials.
Voice:	Acronyms are very helpful when the name of something is very long.
Range/Habitat:	Found especially in governmental, medical, and military environments, acronyms are a verbal and written shorthand. When well-known, they are perfectly permissible to use. Often, the first time the complete name is mentioned, you will see it written out in its full length. The acronym should then follow, inside parentheses. Every subsequent mention of the name will then be in the form of the acronym. Because of this convention, you will find many defining acronyms crouched between the left arc and the right arc of parentheses.
Examples:	*DONSA* (Day of No Scheduled Activity)

*GAFF (*Government Accommodation of Financial Fraud)

GRAS (Generally Regarded As Safe)

INCUR (Industrial Negligence with Commonly Utilized Resources)

BOMB (Barrenizing Operations for Military Benefit)

PIPS (Pipeline Incursion through Populated Surroundings)

WICC (Widespread Ignorance of Climate Change)

CHICPEA (Children's Health Investigation, Care and Protection, and Education Association)

The first Day of No Scheduled Activity (DONSA) fell on a Thursday. After that, we had DONSAs every Saturday; most people used the time reading books and letters from home.

While sufficient, long-term research regarding their safety has not occurred, genetically-modified foods have achieved the status of Generally Recognized as Safe (GRAS) and are rife in the food supply. Many organizations, such as the Children's Health Investigation, Care and Protection, and Education Association (CHICPEA) have been questioning this state of affairs for years, but neither CHICPEA nor any other organization has brought the issue before the courts.

The Ampersand

CLASS: Narratopsida
ORDER: Scriberales
FAMILY: Breviaridae
GENUS: *Adiunctio*
SPECIES: *A. necnon*

COMMON NAMES: The *And* Symbol

Ancestral Record/ Pedigree:

The ampersand evolved, not as a mark of punctuation, but as a word transformed into a distinctive symbolic form. It is a ligature—the Latin word, *et* ("and"), whose two letters morphed into a picture with the vertical *t* next to the middle stroke of the *e*. The oldest known fossil of this mark was found in Pompeii, in an incised bit of graffiti on a wall which survived the eruption of Mount Vesuvius in A.D. 79. It was *ET*, with the two letters written together to form a single symbol. Since that early example, the mark has evolved into more of an abstract, curlicue shape as the result of embellishment and modifications by scribes and writers over the centuries.

Description/ Field Marks:

The word, *ampersand*, comes from the shortened spoken phrase, & *per se and*, which meant "this symbol (&) by itself has the meaning of *and*." In early lists of the alphabet, the ampersand followed the letter *Z* and in spoken, rote recitations became "ampersand." The mark in its written form is far removed now from its descent from the Latin *et*. In most fonts, it looks like a voluptuous *8*, with an arm crossing a leg, or a seated person facing right and doing some modified Seal or Boomerang yoga position.

Voice: Writers use ampersands to abbreviate the word, "and."

Range/Habitat: Ampersands are most often found in business, company, or firm names to show the partnership of two or more people. They reside immediately before the last name in the list, with no commas before them. They are also sometimes used to abbreviate the Latin phrase, *et cetera* ("and so forth," "in this way, "&c") though this usage is not as common as the simple "etc." In referring to the collaboration of two authors on a screenplay or script, the Writers' Guild uses the ampersand to indicate that two writers worked together. The word "and" shows that the two authors worked on the script at different times and may not have consulted with one another. In some styles of citation, you will find the ampersand preceding the last author's name when there is more than one author. Additionally, writers often use the ampersand to show that the "and" in a listed element is part of the element's name and not a separator. For example, in a list of music genres, a reader might find the ampersand like this: "Rock, Pop, Country & Western, and Rhythm & Blues."

Examples: *Colwell, Prasher & Craig, Attorneys at Law*

Russ & Sons

R&B (Rhythm and Blues music genre)

B&B (Bed and Breakfast, a type of inn or lodging where breakfast is included in the price)

R&D (Research and Development)

Dent & Daughters

Cash & Alexander (a grocery store chain)

an S&L bank (a savings and loan bank)

Bennington, Isola & Cheetah Hills (a railroad)

(Allston & Browning, 1989) (authors and date of publication)

Angle Brackets

CLASS:	Narratopsida
ORDER:	Scriberales
FAMILY:	Interpunctidae
GENUS:	*Amplector*
SPECIES:	*A. cruscaprarum*

Ancestral Record/ Pedigree:

Angle brackets share with quotation marks a common ancestor, the *diple* [see Quotation Marks]. This *diple* was often found in the margins of text to draw the reader's attention to something interesting on an associated line.

Description/ Field Marks:

The left (or left-pointing) angle bracket lies on its side with its tip pointing to the left; the right (or right-pointing) angle bracket lies on its side with its tip pointing right. Do not be confused between these brackets and other almost identical-looking marks: *guillemets*; chevrons; lesser than and greater than symbols; rewind and fast forward symbols on some media devices; and the *bras* and *kets* of physics. This confusion will not occur if you pay attention to habitat or context. In addition, with careful observation of the markings, you will also be able to detect the slight differences. *Guillemets* are a little smaller than angle brackets. They serve as double arrows on either side of a quote in some non-local environments. The lesser than and greater than symbols are lighter in color and more flattened than true angle brackets. In addition, their angles are more acute. The *bra-ket* angles are more obtuse than true angle brackets.

Range/Habitat: In non-English quotes, you can often find *guillemets* (double angle brackets, in a pinch) behaving in the same way as quotation marks to enclose direct speech. In the location of mathematics or quantum mechanics, it is not uncommon to see something like the right angle bracket, or *ket*, used in notations to indicate column vectors or quantum states. The left angle in the case of quantum mechanics is called a *bra* but, as noted above, is more obtuse.

You can now also find angle brackets as part of an email address on the internet. Because people do not think like computers, they often like to see a displayed name, but a computer program will read only the actual email address which is enclosed by angle brackets. Angle brackets have a history with computers and a still-strong modern affiliation with them. In the early days of computing, the right-pointing angle bracket could be seen identifying replies in email threads.

Examples: >> *When do you want to meet?*
> *Thursday at 2:30. Will that work?*
>> *Sounds good. See you then.*

Lucy Bosphorus <lbosphorus@someservice.com>

The computer reads *emailname@someservice.com*

11

The Apostrophe

CLASS: Narratopsida
ORDER: Scriberales
FAMILY: Interpunctidae
GENUS: *Subpono*
SPECIES: *S. vestigiumfluitan*

Ancestral history/ Pedigree:

The apostrophe in English is a descendant of the apostrophe of French, which was discovered by Geoffroy Tory in 1529. He used it in place of a vowel letter to show an elision, the leaving out or slurring in pronunciation. Consequently, *la heure* became *l'heure*. The English imported the apostrophe and used it to mark omission, as well, when letters or sounds smashed together. Often, there was a spoken/written correspondence. For some words, however, such as *won't* for *will not*, the written elision created a sound change. One wonders which came first, the change in writing or the change in pronunciation? In any case, the first use of the apostrophe was for contractions. Its name comes ultimately from Greek, through Latin and French.

The use of the apostrophe to show possession has a more debated and complicated history, the end result of which is still a mark that shows "something is missing," just like its original meaning in French. Whether the missing something was the old noun ending of *-es*, or *-is*, or *-ys*, or *his*—all of which were ways to show the possessive, or genitive, case—the apostrophe was the stand-in. Whenever you read something like "William His Book," you know it is this old form of showing possession or ownership. Some examples border on the ridiculous, since the *his*, no matter the gender of the noun, was possessive. One scholar (Thomas Pyles) found this 1607 example in the Oxford English Dictionary (OED) in 1964: "Mrs. Sands his maid." Today we would employ the apostrophe thus: "Mrs. Sands's maid." In some contexts, the apostrophe is employed to denote the measurement of feet.

Description/
Field Marks:

Apostrophes look very much like commas, but their habitat is quite different. Apostrophes float like buoys on a tide, with each one at the top of the line as a curved mark. Because an apostrophe looks exactly the same as a closing single quotation mark, it can easily be misidentified.

Voice:

Writers use an apostrophe for two main purposes. The first is to create a contraction, which is the removal of a letter, letters, numbers, or a word. A writer will then add an apostrophe and close up the gap left by the omission to shorten the word. Consequently, when you see an apostrophe in this situation, you know that something is missing. Be careful, however, as the second purpose of apostrophes is to show possession or ownership. Most of the time, you can tell this is the case when an apostrophe is followed by an *s* (for most singular nouns, and for plural nouns that do not end in *s*). If the noun is plural and ends in *s*, you will see the apostrophe after the *s* to show possession. Compound nouns can be a little confusing, but not if you remember that the last word *only* in the group shows possession and has the apostrophe.

Range/Habitat:

Apostrophes are very often found before and after the letter *s* when used to show possession. Something you will always see in the case of the apostrophe that shows possession is another noun somewhere after the one with the apostrophe. These punctuation marks are also prone to resting between an *n* and a *t*, as well, when they are expressing the omission of a letter or letters. They also can often be seen between the subject pronoun (*he, she, I,* for examples) and two *l*'s (as in *I'll* for *I will*) or before *re,* a common contraction of *are,* as in *they're, you're,* and *we're.* 'Tis hard to figure out sometimes! Another location frequented by apostrophes is between a *she,* a *he,* or an *it* and the letter *s.* When this is the case, the apostrophe has replaced the word *is* or the verb part, *has,* for a contraction. Apostrophes are also found with abbreviated dates.

Examples: *Russ's ambition will get him far if he tempers it with consideration of others.*

She couldn't shake off his relentless pursuit. (could not)

It's 12 o'clock (12 of the clock*)*

He'd have done anything to steal the necklace. (would)

The oak tree was 66' tall.

The Everses' house is located in Ankh.

Arden Evers's brother's name is Oliver.

Both of their daughters-in-law's careers are related to science.

It was the worst flood since the one in '59.

Whish and Whosh's nest was in the tree branch directly above where Arden stood.

Comments: In writing, you should not see an apostrophe of possession after an inanimate object. If you do, it is because a writer did not recast the sentence to prevent this unhealthy proximity. This kind of apostrophe/inanimate object positioning is perfectly acceptable in spoken English, however, and sometimes unavoidable when writing.

The antidote's excessive cost was far too much for her to pay. (unhealthy proximity)

The excessive cost of the antidote was far too much for her to pay. (better and healthy)

As Exotics: *The Evers' house is located in Ankh.*

Arden Evers' brothers name is Oliver.

Both of their daughters-in-laws' careers are related to science.

This old riddle is a good example of the apostrophe and *s* to show possession:

Brothers and sisters I have none,
But that man's father is my father's son.

It's possible to over-use the possessive apostrophe, but sometimes its use is necessary for conveying complicated relational meaning:

My brother's friend's sister's son is very artistic.

Comments: There are many possessive adjectives in English, and they do *not* congregate with nor are they friendly to apostrophes. Often people confuse these possessive adjectives with their same-sounding contractions:

Possessive Adjective	Contraction
its	*it's*
their	*they're*
your	*you're*

There is also some confusion with the pronoun, "whose," and the contraction, "who's." If you remember that the latter one is a contraction, and if you remember that missing letters are quickly in-filled by apostrophes, you will more easily select or understand the correct form.

whose   *who's (who is)*   *who's (who has)*

That the above pronouns and contractions sound exactly the same is what adds to the confusion. However, another good way to tell them apart is that, after a possessive adjective, you will *always* find the presence of a noun, but when there is an apostrophe for a contraction, you might see something else (or a noun, also, so be careful!). Keep in mind that in formal writing, you are least likely to find contractions at all.

They are the pair of owls whose nest contained a wad of steel wool.

Arden is the young girl who's had some difficult experiences mixed with remarkable ones.

The Requisitions Officer is the person who's in charge of ordering material and materiel for the fort.

As Exotics: *They are the pair of owls who's nest contained a wad of steel wool.*

Arden is the young girl whose had some difficult experiences mixed with remarkable ones.

The Requisitions Officer is the person whose in charge of ordering material and materiel for the fort.

The most mistreated word in the English language is, by a majority of accounts, the possessive adjective, *its.* Here is one way to avoid adding to the abuse: The *only* time you will see an apostrophe between the *t* and *s* of this word is when it is a contraction (the apostrophe stands in for missing letters). One of these contractions shortens "it is" to *it's*; the other shortens "it has" to *it's*. In the former case, you will most often see a capital *I* since the word, nine times out of ten, will be at the beginning of a sentence, with the *It* being a subject. In the latter case (the contraction of "it has"), writers only use the contracted form when the "has" is showing tense, or time. They never use the contracted form when the "has" is the actual verb. Consequently, when you spot *it's* for "it has," you will see the past participle form (or third form) of a verb after this contraction.

Examples:

People tell me that it's taken far too long for me to repair my place of business.

It's been very hot in Jayenel for the past two years.

It's time to go swimming!

My vivarium is very large; it has many glass tanks in which I raise the marks of punctuation.

As Exotics:

People tell me that its taken far too long for me to repair my place of business.

Its been very hot in Jayenel for the past two years.

Its time to go swimming!

My vivarium is very large; it's many glass tanks in which I raise the marks of punctuation.

The Asterisk

CLASS: Narratopsida
ORDER: Scriberales
FAMILY: Graphidae
GENUS: *Hypomnema*
SPECIES: *H. stella*

COMMON NAME: The Star Symbol

Description/ Field Marks:	**The asterisk looks like a six-pointed snowflake or star. In fact, its name comes from the Latin root for star, *-aster-* or *-astr-*.**
Voice:	We see the asterisk in two different environments. In one, the mark comes after a word or bit of information and tells the reader that there is a footnote—or extra, qualifying information—at the bottom of the page. This is the use that means "Read the fine print!" when seen in any advertisement. The second use of the asterisk is in more informal writing. It replaces letters in a profane or swear word that a writer wants to "clean up" or sanitize.
Range/Habitat:	Asterisks are found above the line of text, like little stars. There should be a matching one at the bottom of the page if it is being used for its footnote purpose. If replacing letters in a swear word, a writer will include the first letter of the swear word, and from that hint

and a knowledge of swear words the reader can then figure out what the full word is.

Examples: *A new roof will cost nine thousand dinras.**

When I started to slide off of the roof, the thought in my head was "d***!" However, because of my young audience, I yelled aloud: "Oh, my!"

*if paid for, in full, in all cash prior to the commencement of labor.

The *At* Sign

CLASS:	Narratopsida
ORDER:	Scriberales
FAMILY:	Ligaturidae
GENUS:	*Enumeratio*
SPECIES:	*E. mensio*

COMMON NAMES: *At* Symbol, Commercial *At*, *At* Rate Symbol, *At* Site Symbol, Ampersat, Arobase, Arroba

Description/ Field Marks:	**The *at* sign, @, looks a little bit like a small letter *a* inside a letter *e* or a small letter *a* with a counter-clockwise circle almost completely surrounding it.**
Voice:	The *at* sign is used to designate the price of each item or its rate in a ledger or on an invoice. It means "at the rate of" in this context. It can also show the meaning of "at the site/location of."
Range/Habitat:	Originally found in accounting records, on vouchers, in ledgers, and on commercial invoices, the *at* sign has recently been seen migrating into the habitat of email addresses. This has prompted the coinage of "ampersat" to differentiate it from the older "at the rate of" meaning. One can now also see the *at* sign in the field of sporting events where it is used to show at which location a game is being played. In this instance, its meaning is "at the site of." The visiting team is listed first.

Examples:
 5 Bottles Fruckie Corn Soda @ $2.00 (= $10.00)

Notice how the above has a much different meaning than the one below:

5 Bottles Fruckie Corn Soda at $2.00 (= $2.00)

bobbobesobee@countyjail.gov

Ankh Mini Minnows @ Eufaula Small Fries

Brackets

CLASS: Narratopsida
ORDER: Scriberales
FAMILY: Interpunctidae
GENUS: *Amplecti*
SPECIES: *A. explicandum*

COMMON NAMES: Square Brackets

Ancestral Record/ Pedigree:
This mark, named from the same root as "braces" or "breeches," holds a section of writing together just as brackets from a hardware store can hold up a shelf, or bookends hold books between them, or braces hold teeth in position.

Description/ Field Marks:
Brackets have two forms: the left bracket and the right bracket. They are similar in appearance to parentheses but instead of being gently curved are squared. Brackets, like quotation marks and (traditionally) parentheses, generally mate for life.

Voice:
Writers use brackets in a similar way to how they use parentheses because brackets impart extra information, or add an authorial or editorial comment to a text. They are mainly used to insert explanatory material or instructions, to mark where a passage was omitted from original material, or to mark changes in quotations.

Range/Habitat: Brackets are found on either side of things. Very often, they can be found on either side of the Latin word, *sic* ("in this way" or "just as" or "so" or "thus") after a quote or part of a text where an original mistake is being reproduced. Used in this way, the [*sic*] tells a reader that the mistake is not that of the writer/quoter but was made by the original source. You will often see brackets on either side of an ellipsis [see The Ellipsis]. In this position, the brackets indicate that material has been omitted.

Bracketed comments inserted into a quote indicate when the original has been modified for clarity. They can also be observed setting off a grammatical modification of a quoted original statement. In translated text, note that brackets are used to avoid ambiguity. When nested parentheses are needed, brackets often replace the inner pair of parentheses. If there are deeper levels of parenthetical material—when more nesting is needed— you can observe how the parentheses and brackets alternate. This nesting, or enclosure, is a little like Matryoshka dolls, nesting boxes, or Fukuruma in the way parts of sentences can be placed, parenthetically, in other parts of sentences. Too much nesting, however, can be confusing. Most writers, if they can, try to avoid having more than one level of enclosure as mixing so many parentheses and brackets can wind up in a tangled mess.

In the environment of mathematical equations, brackets can be spotted grouping together certain elements, with parentheses grouping together others.

Examples: *"Regardless of the findings from scientists the world over, we will continue to go about our business and follow prevailing economic models as usual. Global warming and anthropogenic climate change is [sic] not genuine."*

"Regardless of the findings [. . .], anthropogenic climate change is not genuine."

[To be continued]

When the boar sow sniffed the contents of it [Ennui's sack], she started to sneeze uncontrollably.

*Many modern manufactories are still sources of **indentured servitude** [emphasis added].*

No actions were taken by any of the organizations present, which was not surprising since the hosting group (Widespread Ignorance of Climate Change [WICC]) firmly believes in the status quo.

Males crickets can be identified by the presence of an angled pair of long cerci [spikes] at the end of their abdomens.

Please solve the following equation: 4[x–(3–2x)]+5=3(x+11)

Capital Letters

CLASS:	Narratopsida
ORDER:	Scriberales
FAMILY:	Litteridae
GENUS:	*Protospecios*
SPECIES:	*P. orsus*

Ancestral Record/ Pedigree:

Capital letters used to be more common than they are today. Before the middle of the 1700s, when capitalization became more standardized (from Alexander Pope and Noah Webster, primarily), writers often used capital letters for all nouns or to emphasize important words, which created a "shoutiness" in their texts. Today, the use of capital letters is more regulated as the standard is now sentence case (where the first letter of a sentence is capitalized). The word, "capital" is derived from the Latin, *caput*, meaning "head," which has led to many related words in English with the meaning of "most important" or "chief." As an example, a capital city is the most important, and when you wear a cap, where do you put it?

Description/ Field Marks:

Capital letters—also known as uppercase letters— can most easily be spotted at the head of a sentence [see Lowercase Letters]. Each letter of the alphabet has two forms: the uppercase and the lowercase. Like a wild turkey tom announcing and defending his posse of hens, jennies, jakes, and poults, capital letters announce and lead their subsequent lowercase letters in a sentence. They are taller than lowercase letters and, usually, more angular.

Voice: Capital letters are very useful in helping to identify new sentence beginnings and to show that a noun is not common but rather a proper (named) one.

Range/Habitat: As already noted, one can find capital letters at the beginning of a sentence and as the pronoun *I*. However, there are many other locations where they can be spotted by a careful observer: the names of individuals, tribes, clans, and ethnic groups; the names of places or physical locations, such as countries, cities, towns, mountains, and rivers; the names of languages; the names of ships, aircraft, and trains; the names of religions and other belief systems; the names of political parties; the names of gods and personifications; the names of days of the week and months of the year (but not seasons); the names of holidays and celebrations; the names of planets and other celestial bodies (though not the earth, moon, or sun when used generally). Titles and honorifics also are capitalized, as are national and regional adjectives, product brand names, capitonyms (words which change their meaning between capitalized and uncapitalized usage, such as "march" and "March," "turkey" and "Turkey," and "liberal" and "Liberal"); compass directions that refer to geographical regions ("the West," "the Northeast"); and the titles of books, films, specific courses at a school, songs, or television programs. Any one of these is a good location for sighting capital letters.

Examples: *Her best friend moved to Eufaula.*

Every year, the town of Ankh holds the Calvatia Festival.

Mr. Dander is an important customer of mine, and his orders are crucial to the success of my business.

Jupiter is the largest planet in our solar system; its diameter is eleven times that of Earth (or the earth).

The name of Mr. Psyllenquay's boat was Aviso.

Cedro Wooley drove the tractor as fast as it would go and, once they got to the coffee shop, offered to buy her a Fruckie soda.

The Colon

CLASS:	Narratopsida
ORDER:	Scriberales
FAMILY:	Interpunctidae
GENUS:	*Maximita*
SPECIES:	*M. notitia*

Ancestral Record/ Pedigree:
The colon is one of three modern punctuation marks that evolved from the three dots that Aristophanes, a scholar and the chief of staff at the library of Alexandria, used in the 3rd century B.C.E to annotate the hundreds of Greek scrolls that the library contained. Greeks had long written their texts in all capital letters (*uncial*, a majuscule script) without spacing or punctuation between. THELETTERSINATEXTRANTOGETHER and, consequently, were difficult to read. Aristophanes used dots at the middle, bottom, or top of each line to break verses with pauses. For a short pause, a *stigmè mésē* dot (a *komma*) was placed mid-level (•) Longer pauses were marked with a *hypostigmé* dot (a *kolon*) placed level with the bottom of the text (.) For very long pauses (*periodos*), a *stigmè teleía* dot near the top of the line of text (•) was inserted. This high dot stood for the end of a sentence and was a precursor to our modern period. However, at the time, the marks indicated lengths of pauses for speaking and had nothing to do with syntax or grammatical boundaries. People

could add the dots to text so they would know how to read it aloud. An updated version of Aristophanes's punctuation dots was used by Isidore of Seville (in Spain) in A.D. 700. Isidore initiated the connecting of the dots to *meaning* and grammar (instead of pauses). Over the years, Aristophanes's system evolved yet more, with the period dropping to the bottom of the line, the comma getting a curve and also dropping to the bottom of the line, and the colon getting an extra dot.

Description/ Field Marks:	**The colon is easily recognizable by its two dots, one directly above the other.**
Voice:	Writers use a colon to create suspense. It signals that an example, list, quotation, explanation, or rule will follow. It basically says: "I'm about to tell you more about what I have just said."
Range/Habitat:	Colons follow independent clauses to introduce information that explains that clause. You will also most likely be able to find a colon in these locations: separating an hour from minutes in a notation of time; after the greeting (salutation) in a business or formal letter; separating the title of something from its subtitle; separating a Biblical chapter from a verse or a Qur'anic *surah* from an *ayah*; separating chapters and lines of other religious and historical texts, such as the Nihon Shoki, the Holy Tanakah, the Gura Granth Sahib, the Dhammapada, the Book of Mormon, and the Bhagavad Gita. Colons also introduce a list. In this environment, it follows a noun.
Examples:	*The train will depart at 10:48 a.m.*
	Dear Mr. Dander:
	The Bristlecone Pine: Witness to the Ages
	(Num. 31:7-18, King James Version)

(Al-Isra, 17:16, Qur'an)

(2Nephi 5:21-25, The Book of Mormon)

*The Northern Mockingbird has a repertoire of up to
four hundred songs that imitate what it hears in its
environment: other birds, frogs, car alarms, insects,
machinery.*

*Tomorrow, I need to do several maintenance tasks: remove
the Apostrophes from their tank; scrub the inside glass of the
tank with distilled white vinegar; rinse and thoroughly dry
the glass; refill the tank with fresh water; and then return
all the Apostrophes to it.*

He ordered several marks: some z's and some dinra signs.

I have one word for you: photovoltaics.

As Exotics: *The Northern Mockingbird has a repertoire of up to 400
songs that imitate: other birds, frogs, car alarms, insects,
machinery.*

*Tomorrow, I need to: remove the Apostrophes from their
tank; scrub the inside glass of the tank with distilled white
vinegar; rinse and thoroughly dry it; refill the tank with
fresh water; and then return all the Apostrophes to it.*

He ordered: some z's and some dinra signs.

The Comma

CLASS:	Narratopsida
ORDER:	Scriberales
FAMILY:	Interpunctidae
GENUS:	*Amplius*
SPECIES:	*A. ordo*

Ancestral Record/ Pedigree:

The modern comma evolved from a point or dot ("*punctus*") placed on a line of text to signify for a reader to take a short pause when reading aloud [see The Colon]. In ancient times, much reading was done this way. Aristophanes, who lived over 2,300 years ago and was head of the famous Library of Alexandria in Hellenic Egypt, created a system of three dots to denote pauses. A short pause was referred to in the Greek as the *komma*. Originally, the dot for this shortest pause was located in the middle of the line. However, an Italian writer in the 12th century, Buoncompagno da Signa, altered the existing punctuation of Aristophanes and that of Isidore of Seville with his own system of a slash (*suspensivus*) and a dash (*planus*). The former represented a pause, just as Aristophanes's middle dot had, and by the 1400s the dot and the slash were used interchangeably. Over time, the mark dropped to the bottom of the line and became curved—the form that modern commas display today.

Description/ Field Marks:	**Commas are everywhere, so it is very easy to find them. In fact, the comma is more widespread in distribution than the period. A comma looks exactly like an apostrophe except that it prefers to live in the understory of a sentence, at the bottom of the line of text. Apostrophes are aquatic surface feeders; commas are terrestrial.**
Voice:	When writers join two complete ideas or independent clauses, they use a comma and a coordinator (coordinating conjunction) to join them together. However, the most common function of the comma is to delineate or set off extra information from the basic subject-verb-(object) form of a sentence. Commas also serve as an indicator species for the main subjects of a sentence or of an independent clause. Like in the web of life, every element of a sentence depends on a co-existent relationship with other elements. The presence of commas indicates a favorable environment for extra information, pauses, and sentence subjects.
Range/Habitat:	Extra information can be at the end of a sentence. In this case, you can spot a comma immediately to the left of this information. It is very possible, however, that the extra information (such as the "however" in this sentence) will be *between* two commas.

Many people who use commas follow the edict: "Put a comma after an introductory phrase or after a dependent clause that begins a sentence." My advice is a little more straightforward and memorable, I hope: "You have the greatest chance of finding a comma if you look before the subject of an independent clause (the main subject)." A comma immediately precedes the main subject if *any* words come before that subject. Now, I realize that "after an introductory phrase or after a dependent clause" and "immediately before the main subject" put the comma in exactly the same location, but to my mind it is much easier to remember the position of the comma the second way than the first way (that of many grammar books). If *anything* comes before the main subject—a single word, even (such as a transition or signal word)—you should see a comma grazing quietly in front of that subject.

You can almost always be assured of finding a comma after the greeting of an informal or personal letter, and you will also see a comma after the closing of correspondence. This closing is commonly the word, "Sincerely."

Usually, you will not see a comma in a series with only two elements. However, in a series of three elements joined with a coordinator, you should be able to spot a comma before the "and" before the last element. Many writers do this to avoid confusion.

If you should be fortunate enough to come across a sentence where the subject and its verb are separated by a phrase (a group of words without a subject and its verb), this is an example of extra information, and you will see a comma on either side of this phrase.

Writers also use commas to set off a quotation from words that introduce or identify the source of the quote. Because of this, you will often find these marks somewhere near the verb 'said', 'told', or before an opening quotation mark or a closing one.

Examples:

They ran up the stairs, and Mastiff threw herself against the door.

The cricket struggled in the web. Then, he pleaded with the spiders to release him.

The cricket struggled in the web; then, he pleaded with the spiders to release him.

Struggling in the web, the cricket pleaded with the spiders to release him.

Many birds, to protect their young, will fly away from the nest and feign injury in order to distract a predator.

The Newtamee Herald-Tribune orders many hyphens, necessary punctuation marks for the masthead of the town's newspaper.

She had only a few items: some oak cakes, a toy gun and its two D-cell batteries, and the clothes she was wearing.

I raise apostrophes, commas, periods, em and ens, parentheses, and many other marks.

When a mourning dove takes off in flight, it emits a sharp whistling or whinnying sound—not a vocalization but, rather, a high-pitched vibration made by its wings. Its vocalization is a hollow, mournful cooing that is often, and erroneously, thought to be that of an owl.

Dear Claudia,

"It is not often that such a big idea can be expressed in so few words," he said, "but 'as goes the nation' might be one example."

"Understanding is a way of making yourself ready," Darla told her.

Sincerely,
Albert Drosoph

As Exotics: *They ran up the stairs and Mastiff threw herself against the door.*

He struggled in the web, then he pleaded with the spiders to release him.

He struggled in the web. Then he pleaded with the spiders to release him.
Struggling in the web he pleaded with the spiders to release

him.

The Newtamee Herald-Tribune orders many hyphens necessary punctuation marks for the masthead of the town's newspaper.

She had only a few items, some oak cakes, a toy gun and its two D-cell batteries, and the clothes she was wearing.

"It is not often that such a big idea can be expressed in so few words" he said "but 'as goes the nation' might be one example."

The fire burned through many acres, and caused people and animals to flee.

Knave told her, that he could give her direction.

She wanted to get back to Ankh where she was from.

She wanted to get back to the town, where she was from.

My vivarium where I raise punctuation marks is hardly ever visited by people, most of my business is by mail order.

The cricket was a bit full of himself, however, he helped Arden tremendously with his chirps.

The Dash

CLASS: Narratopsida
ORDER: Scriberales
FAMILY: Interpunctidae
GENUS: *Amplius*
SPECIES: *A. retractu*

COMMON NAME: Em Dash

Description/
Field Marks:

The dash looks like a horizontal line—remarkably similar to the hyphen. However, it is located in different environments and has an entirely different function. Careful observation of field marks and context will help you with identification. For example, it is twice as long as a hyphen. The hyphen connects while the dash separates. In function and location, the dash more closely resembles the comma and parentheses. It is a very distinctive mark and not easy to miss.

Voice:

Writers use the dash to insert a comment or to highlight material in a sentence. The dash also can set off an interruption—an abrupt break—or introduce extra information, such as a noun renaming a noun, or a summary.

Range/Habitat:

This mark can be found going about singly or in pairs. It can be found in the same locations as parentheses but has much stronger character. Because it sets off extra information, two dashes are often seen— one on either side of the "broken" text with no extra space separating them from the letters.

Examples: *The dash also can set off an interruption—an abrupt break—or introduce extra information—such as a noun renaming a noun, or a summary.*

The very air we breathe is a legacy of the ancient, living world—the exhalations from blue-green algae (cyanobacteria) over thousands of millions of years.

The Decimal Point

CLASS: Narratopsida
ORDER: Scriberales
FAMILY: Enumeratidae
GENUS: *Signum*
SPECIES: *S. decem*

COMMON NAMES: Point, Dot

Description/ **The decimal point looks exactly like a period and**
Field Marks: **inhabits the same strata of a written line, but its**
function is very different.

Voice: As its name implies (*deca-* or *dec-* is a prefix that
means "ten" in Greek), people use this mark to
designate tenths. It is often pronounced "point."

Range/Habitat: This mark can be found in the vicinity of numbers,
specifically numbers that are fractions of an amount.
Consequently, it is closely related to the percent sign,
and often in a location where you would see one the
other can also often be spotted. For example, 1% could
just as well be .01, and $.10 is less than a whole dinra
(or dollar, depending on where you are [see The Dollar
Sign]. The distribution of the decimal point mimics
that of fractions. While in some areas of the world it
is used as a placeholder after thousands ($1.000,00,
for example), in our more local environment a comma

commands that position ($1,000.00).

Examples: *The voltage of a D-cell battery is 1.5V.*

               *The auto-ignition temperature of bond paper is 238.8
               degrees Celsius; that of an oak sapling is 260 degrees Celsius.*

               She found $.75 in coins on the path.

               The war cost the taxpayers over $1.7 trillion.

Comments: Remember that if you are in the habitat of numbers
               and fractions, what you are most likely observing is
               a decimal point, not a period. Location can be very
               helpful to you for knowing which of these marks you
               are looking at. I once used periods instead of decimal
               points in an electronic ledger, and all of my calculations
               were ruined.

The Dollar Sign

CLASS: Narratopsida
ORDER: Scriberales
FAMILY: Enumeratidae
GENUS: *Adcudo*
SPECIES: *A. pecunia*

COMMON NAMES: Dollar Symbol, Peso Sign, Peso Symbol, Dinra Sign

Ancestral record/ Pedigree:	Historically, this mark may have come from a ligature (combination) of *p* and *s* written together to show "peso," the commanding currency of the Spanish Empire from the 16th to the 19th century.
Description/ Field Marks:	**The dollar sign looks like a capital letter *S* with one or two vertical lines through it.**
Voice:	A graphic symbol used as a shorthand for currency or amounts of money, the dollar sign is used in many countries, even ones that do not use the word, "dollar," as a name for their currency.
Range/Habitat:	Over thirty countries in the world use this graphic symbol for their currencies. Dollar signs can most often be seen resting on the left side of money amounts, but in some locations it rests on the right side.

In cartoons, when people are illustrated with dollar signs in their eyes, it usually means they are greedy or, at the very least, money-oriented.

Examples: *Dander Industries regularly orders dollar signs to show the $23 million in profit they make each month.*

Dollars to dinras, the symbol, "$" is often vocalized as "cha-ching" (an onomatopoeia, *or sound representation, of an old-fashioned cash register ringing up a sale).*

The Ellipsis

CLASS: Narratopsida
ORDER: Scriberales
FAMILY: Interpunctidae
GENUS: *Subpono*
SPECIES: *S. semita*

COMMON NAMES: The Ellipsis Mark, The Elliptical Mark, Ellipsis Dots, Ellipsis Points, Dot-Dot-Dot (colloquially), Points of Ellipsis, Ellipses, Suspension Points

Ancestral Record/ Pedigree: Not to be confused with Kepler's ellipses of planetary orbits, or eccentric mechanical cams, or the trammel of Archimedes, the modern ellipsis as related to writing and reading was probably first employed as a mark to show omission of text by publisher Thomas East, who, in 1588, brought out an edition of Terence's play, *Andria* (Terence was a former Roman slave who became a playwright). While in this old text a series of hyphens showed the omission, after this appearance in 1588, the marks evolved into a series of (three) dots to show omission, an incomplete thought, or a silence of some kind. These marks quickly caught on, though until the 18th century the idea of "something omitted here" could be shown equally by hyphens or dashes. The word, *ellipsis*, comes from Greek (*elleipsis*, from *elleipein*, "to fall short").

Description/ Field Marks:	**The field marks of the ellipsis consist of three dots (looking a lot like periods) in a horizontal row at the bottom of a line of text. These dots are separated from each other and from the text on either side by spaces.** Perhaps people erroneously apply the plural word, "ellipses," to this single mark because of the plurality of dots, but the mark is considered a single element of punctuation. The plural form may be a shorthand of joining the adjective "ellipsis" with its plural noun, "dots." Another theory for this error is that the punctuation ellipsis has been confused with the ellipsis of shape, for if you intersect a cone in two different locations with an angled plane, you will have two ellipses.
Voice:	Writers use the ellipsis to show where they have intentionally and consciously omitted something from a text or quotation or where the original passage was missing or illegible. This usage must not alter the original meaning, however. Depending on its context and placement in a sentence, an ellipsis can also indicate an unfinished thought, a hesitation, a mysterious voice, or an awkward silence. Other uses are to suggest faltering or fragmented speech or ideas, which are caused by confusion, uncertainty, distress, or insecurity. The use of an ellipsis to trail off at the end of a sentence has a special name: an *aposiopesis*.
Range/Habitat:	An ellipsis is often bracketed [see Brackets]. When the ellipsis comes at the end of a sentence, it is followed by a period, so you will see a "train" of four dots. In locations or contexts of mathematics, an ellipsis is often used to mean "and so forth."
Examples:	*There were many items in the cart, all of which were covered by a camouflaged tarp.* (original) *There were many items in the cart . . . covered by a camouflaged tarp.* (omitted)

There were many items in the cart [. . .] covered by a camouflaged tarp. (omitted)

"But I thought you said . . . I mean . . . it seems not true at all."

1, 2, 3, 4 . . . 100.

They began to recite the alphabet (a, b, c . . .).

They began to recite a, b, c . . . .

The Exclamation Point

CLASS: Narratopsida
ORDER: Scriberales
FAMILY: Interpunctidae
GENUS: *Clausula*
SPECIES: *C. mirandumensatus*

COMMON NAMES: Exclamation Mark, Bang, Shriek Mark, Screamer

Ancestral Record/ Pedigree:
Some paleo-graphologists believe that the origins of this mark consisted of a ligature of the Latin *io*, meaning "exclamation of joy." The *i* was written above the *o*. Another theory is that the *i* and *o* came from a shorthand of the Latin word, *interiectio*, meaning "interjection," where the first letter was stacked above the last letter. The first manuscript to employ this mark is believed to be Coluccio Salutati's, *The Nobility of Law and Medicine,* from 1399. Earlier in the 14th century, however, Iacopo Alpoleio da Urbisaglia wrote *Ars punctuani* or *The Art of Punctuating* (some scholars attribute authorship to a man named Petrarca). Regardless of the book's author, however, its text made mention of, and people subsequently started to use, an "admiration point," which was a translation of Iacopo's term, *punctus admirativus*. It looked like two points with a tilted line above them. When this "sign of admiration" or "note of admiration" migrated to printing in the 15th century, it was used to show emphasis or

a sense of wonderment. The term "exclamation point," or "exclamation mark," was in use by the 1600s. The final shape of this mark developed with the advent of printing press type in the mid-15th century.

Description/ Field Marks:	**The mark as it looks today consists of a single dot at the bottom of a line of text. The dot is capped by a straight vertical line.**

Voice:

Writers use this mark to express surprise, shock, and excitement. It is comparable to a shout or a scream—maybe of wonderment, still— but most often it denotes excitement over some trivial event. For a long period of history, the exclamation point was little used, but its prevalence has increased in more modern times even as past editors tried to eradicate it or, at the least, keep its rabbit-like fecundity in check. The prevailing belief of these editors was that the mark showed a failure of writing skill. Their program of "exclamaticide" was so effective that the mark was once on the brink of extinction. Lately, however, it has surged in both population and popularity, with its steadily increasing use primarily the result of emailing and, inferentially, failed writing skill.

Range/Habitat:

You can find this punctuation mark in advertisements, mostly, but also in many emails and phone texts. The recent over-exploitation of this exclamatory resource is unprecedented.

Examples:

Big Sale!

20% Off All Items in Stock!

Warning! May Cause Blindness!

We Make Better Britches!!!

The Hyphen

CLASS:	Narratopsida
ORDER:	Scriberales
FAMILY:	Interpunctidae
GENUS:	*Ecfio*
SPECIES:	*E. glutino*

Ancestral Record/
Pedigree:

The hyphen is an old mark, but writers did not fully start to exploit its benefits until the mid-1500s. Some paleo-graphologists, though, claim it dates back to at least 70 B.C., when it was used by the Greek grammarian, Dionysium Thrax. Hyphens became increasingly popular in print from the 1570s onward. The name, *hyphen*, was not recorded until the early 1600s and came from an ancient Greek word meaning "together." It served the purpose of joining parts of words that had been separated because they were unable to fit on a single line of text. Johannes Gutenberg, in his 1455 42-line-per-page Bible, freely used a related species to our modern hyphen. His was a double, stacked hyphen, inclined to the right at a 60-degree slant. Later on, the hyphen evolved into a single line and became horizontal, not slanted. The hyphen is still used in this way today.

Description/
Field Marks:

The hyphen is a single, short horizontal line that comes between word parts or at breaks in words at their syllabic nodes at the end of a page line. Hyphens

look very much like dashes, but they are of a differing genus. Hyphens are in the genus *Ecfio* and dashes are in the genus *Amplius*. Careful observation will show that the dash is twice as long as the hyphen. Additionally, hyphens and dashes do very different things and are found in different habitats.

Voice: Hyphens connect or separate words or syllables of words. Writers use them in compound words, to join prefixes to other words, and to show word (syllable) breaks when the whole word doesn't fit in a line of text.

Range/Habitat: Hyphens are very useful characters, but they are also very tricky. They seem to insert themselves willy-nilly (there's one!) into the environment. As a historical pattern, many compound adjectives and compound nouns of today started out as separate words and then were joined with a hyphen for awhile before becoming "closed." As an example, the word, "tonight" used to be written as "to night." In between the "open" form and the "closed" (solid) form, the hyphenated form ("to-night") was a way station for awhile. Many modern compound nouns have remained "open" (water cooler, ice cream), but there are many more that have closed up after the hyphen left them (watermelon, email, handwriting). Such is the evolution of language and the fickleness of punctuation marks when their traditional habitat changes or no longer suits them.

Comments: More and more often, hyphens that in the past joined word parts together are disappearing, and the words are becoming a single one. A good example of this is the word "honey bee." For awhile, a hyphen developed a symbiotic relationship with the two words to create "honey-bee." Then, around 2007, the hyphen apparently absconded, so we are now left with "honeybee."

However, many words still retain their hyphens.

One of the most common places to spot hyphens is at word breaks. These occur at the extreme right side of a page where there is not enough room to write the complete word. In this situation, the word must be divided between its syllables. Writers try to avoid having a one- or two-letter part of the word by itself at either the right side of the page or starting the next line. Of course, if a word has only one syllable, you should never see it broken. In addition, the hyphen likes to split double consonants in the middle and comes between some prefixes and their root words.

Most likely, you will see the following:

run-ning	*drop-ping*
demon-strated	*mock-ing-bird*
success-ful	*pre-1990s*
ex-partner	*mourn-ing*

Compound words are unusually rich with hyphens and constitute the second most common place to see them. There are three types: compound adjectives, compound nouns, and compound verbs. Writers use hyphens in these locations to show that the component words have a combined meaning or a relationship between them. Since compound adjectives are the more numerous, and the most confusing, I start my examples with them.

Compound Adjectives

Compound adjectives are constructed in three basic forms: a noun + an adjective; a noun + a participial form; an adjective + a participial form. Do not be alarmed by these terms. A participial form is simply a word with the *-ed* or the *-ing* ending or, if it refers to an irregular verb, the past participle (third form) of that verb. You are very likely to spot a hyphen in the vicinity of many, but not all, compound adjectives.

camera-ready	*custom-built*	*open-mouthed*
carbon-neutral	*muddle-headed*	*quick-thinking*

accident-prone   *power-driven*
sugar-free   *bad-tempered*

Hyphens are also numerous in compound adjectives that are created with the adverb, "well," and a participial form. However, be aware that this is the case only when these compounds as adjectives appear before a noun. If this twinning comes after the noun, you should not see a hyphen.

well-known   *up-to-date*   *friendly-looking*

They export well-known types of armament.

The types of armament that they export are well known.

She gave me an up-to-date account of all that had happened to her.

The account that she gave me about her experiences was up to date.

Mastiff was a friendly-looking dog.

The dog, Mastiff, was friendly looking.

A long-anticipated solution was finally worked out.

The scientists worked out a solution that was long anticipated.

Note: You should not see hyphens in combinations of an adverb which ends in *-ly* plus an adjective.

The antidote was not a readily available drug.

It was a badly written sentence.

Be aware that when hyphens describe ages or lengths of time, they can change the meaning of a sentence very dramatically by their position in the compound adjective:

There were three mile-wide tracts on either side of the river.

There were three-mile-wide tracts on either side of the river.

To clear the forest for the construction of the manufactory, they cut down 250-year-old trees.

To clear the forest for the construction of the manufactory, they cut down 250 year-old trees.

Hyphens sometimes hang or float, with more than one hyphen congregating in a list if the second or third element in the list is the same as the last word of the list:

pro- and anti-government
nineteenth- and twentieth-century immigration patterns
business-men and -women

The yields from Mr. Dander's investments have been consistently six-, seven-, or eight-fold for the past twenty years.

Compound Nouns

Compound nouns are formed from two component nouns and are another location where you might find hyphens (though, of late, more and more hyphens appear to be quitting this kind of environment):

air crew	*air-crew*	*aircrew*
e mail	*e-mail*	*email*
play ground	*play-ground*	*playground*

Since writers are more likely today to select and use compound nouns without hyphens, they must remember to be consistent in their selections and not write "aircrew" on one page and "air-crew" on another.

Compound Verbs

The last compound environment for hyphens is that of verbs. Compound verbs are often formed by two nouns with a hyphen between them:

to booby-trap
to spot-check
to court-martial

Hoping to protect their treasure. they booby-trapped the old shack.

The overseer was careful to spot-check the garments sewn by the workers in the manufactory.

He feared being court-martialed for his offenses against military law.

You should not see hyphens between the parts of two-, three-, or four-word phrasal verbs. In this case, the lack of a hyphen is reserved for the noun form:

*Biofilms **build up** on the tanks' interiors if the tanks are not thoroughly cleaned once a week.*

*Mastiff was able to **break in** the dungeon by throwing herself repeatedly against the door.*

*Wild Boar-Sow persuaded Arden to **stop off** near some trees and admire an amazing spiderweb.*

If a phrasal verb is working as a noun, you should be able to find a hyphen:

*There was a **build-up** of biofilm on the tank's interior.*

*The warehouse was unoccupied at the time of the **break-in**.*

*She made a **stop-off** at the library on her way home from school.*

Prefixes and Suffixes

Certain prefixes when joined to words are excellent places to find hyphens. However, there are many prefixes where hyphens no longer reside or where hyphen presence is variable. Writers usually double-check with dictionaries or style guides [see Editor's Note] because of this variability. The following prefixes are generally good hyphen-viewing areas (areas that are good for the viewing of hyphens, as opposed to good-hyphen viewing areas—areas in which you will see only good hyphens, not the bad ones):

post–   *pre–*   *self–*   *quasi–*
half–   *ex–*   *anti–*   *all–*
co–   *pan–*   *pseudo–*
un– (if followed by a noun with a capital letter)

The suffix, *-elect*, is also a good spot to find a hyphen.

The president-elect made a stirring speech to the crowds.

Also, you can see hyphens with fractions as adjectives:

Three-quarters of the new outbuilding has been constructed.

And with family members:

sister-in-law   *father-in-law*

And with two-word numbers between twenty and ninety-nine whenever they are written out as words:

By the third week, she had already eaten twenty-one of the biscuits she had learned how to make.

Writers use hyphens to show that a word is to be spelled out:

W-O-R-D

In quoted speech, hyphens represent stuttering:

"I would like some p-p-p-potatoes," he stuttered.

And you will see hyphens persevering in places where their departure would make a sentence ambiguous:

re-cover vs. *recover*
re-creation vs. *recreation*
un-ionized vs. *unionized*
re-treat vs. *retreat*
co-op vs. *coop*

In addition, writers will generally use a hyphen to separate words so that similar letters are not together and confusing to the reader's eye. This is especially true for double i's and triple consonants.

bell-like   *anti-intellectual*
wall-less   *semi-invalid*

The hyphen can stand in for the word, "to," in many situations:

We'll work on this from April-July.

He needed to write a 12-16-page booklet for the advertising campaign.

The party lasted from 1-4 p.m.

The hyphen is a mark whose habits and preferences are still being studied as it is an extremely mysterious and versatile character!

As Exotics:

You should not even bother to look for hyphens in the following locations, either because the cut-off syllable is too short, the word has only one syllable, or the hyphen is not at a syllable break:

heal-th   *disa-bled*
talk-ed   *helm-et*
i-dea   *manufa-cture*

Italics

CLASS: Narratopsida
ORDER: Scriberales
FAMILY: Interpunctidae
GENUS: *Proclino*
SPECIES: *P. gravis*

COMMON NAMES: Aldino

Ancestral Record/ In 1501, Venetian Aldus Manutius and his Aldine Press
Pedigree: published the first book printed in a new typeface,
one that imitated the cursive script handwriting
developed in the 1420s by Niccolo de Niccoli. The
typecutter was Francesco da Bologna, whose surname
was Griffo. The new typeface (what we today would
call a font) was sloping, light-bodied, and compact
and so could condense more words on a page. This
allowed for smaller books because the slant of the
Aldine italic allowed for more letters to be crammed
into a line, more words on a page, and fewer pages
in a book. Manutius received exclusive rights to use
his typeface, but its advantages prompted widespread
counterfeit.

Description/ **Italics are a right-slanted, cursive style of print with**
Field Marks: **longer descenders on the letters than regular type. It**
is a flourished style.

Voice: Writers use italics to set words or phrases apart. They give
                    emphasis, mimicking what is called stress in spoken
                    language. Italics are also often used to introduce or define
                    terms, especially technical terms or those that are used
                    in an unusual or different way. Mathematical writers and
                    scientists use italics when they write variables in algebraic
                    equations or symbols of mathematical constants.

Range/Habitat: The titles of books, albums, paintings, plays, and
                    periodicals are often seen in italics. (Works such as a
                    short story, a newspaper article, or a poem that appear
                    within a larger, longer work are not italicized but set
                    off in quotation marks.) You can also find italics in the
                    names of ships, trains, and planes. Non-English words,
                    including the Latin names for living organisms, are
                    another good location for spotting italics. If you see a
                    letter or a number off by itself in a sentence, most likely
                    it will be in italics. Please note that since my example
                    sentences are already in italics, the parts that should be
                    in italics, normally, are shown in regular type—exactly
                    the opposite from how they would usually appear.

Examples: *People always want to write my last name with a* J *instead
                    of with a* D.

                    When Arden saw her name beside the 8 *on the swimming
                    rankings, she knew that she had come in last yet again.*

                    They served a lovely coq au vin.

                    An even *number is one that is a multiple of* 2. *Because
                    humans have two of many body parts (ears, eyes, nostrils,
                    hands, breasts, knees, ankles, feet, hips), even numbers are
                    the "norm." Non-even numbers take on the appellation* odd
                    to show the idea of "different from the norm." The adjective,
                    odd, *in non-mathematical contexts, continues to carry the
                    meaning of "strange," "foreign," "unusual."*

                    *It was James Clerk Maxwell who, in the 1860s, first
                    predicted that light was an electromagnetic wave and
                    computed its speed:* $\lambda \nu = $ c *(where* λ *is the Greek letter,*
                    lambda, *and stands for wavelength of light, and* ν, *the
                    Greek letter* nu, *represents the frequency of the light wave).*

Lowercase Letters

CLASS: Narratopsida
ORDER: Scriberales
FAMILY: Litteridae
GENUS: *Planicia*
SPECIES: *P. trivialis*

Ancestral record/ Pedigree:
Lowercase letters are the most numerous of all written letters [see Capitals]. Even the first person singular pronoun, *I*, used to be lowercase, especially back in the days of Old and Middle English, when it was *ic* or *ich* or variations of these. After the pronoun was reduced to a single letter (a *unigram*), it was very easily misread or lost, so scribes took to increasing its length. Now, *I* is uppercase (majuscule)—but only in English. Other languages keep this self-referential pronoun in lowercase. Does this mean that English-speaking/writing people place more importance on the individual-as-agent? Does it lead to egoism and a too-strong sense of self-regard? Scholars and psychologists say, "No." It is simply a vestige of typographical convenience from the early days of writing and printing.

Description/ Field Marks:
You will find lowercase letters hewing very close to the line. Some, such as *b, d, f, h, k, l,* and *t,* rise above the line; others, such as *g, j, p, q,* and *y,* dip down below it.

Voice: Lowercase letters are the bread and butter of writers. These letters constitute the bulk of everything writers write and everything readers read.

Range/Habitat: More and more, all letters are becoming lowercase— even the pronoun *I*—but this form of writing for texting and emailing often diminishes clarity.

Examples: *just as a piece of writing with all capital letters is difficult to read, so is a piece of writing in only lowercase letters. sometimes, punctuation is not enough to set off the beginnings and ends of sentences. it's much better to use both!*

123

Numbers

CLASS:	Narratopsida
ORDER:	Scriberales
FAMILY:	Enumeratidae
GENUS:	*Mensio*
SPECIES:	*M. privus*

Description/
Field Marks:

Numbers have two forms: Roman and Arabic. It's a good thing that, by convention, we have adopted the Arabic for common use as the Roman numbers, or numerals, are clunky and impossible to use for any kind of mathematical manipulation. The basic building blocks of Arabic numbers look like this: *1, 2, 3, 4, 5, 6, 7, 8, 9,* and *0*. From these elements, one can write any number at all. The basic building blocks for Roman numerals are these: *I* (one), *V* (five), *X* (ten), *L* (fifty), *C* (one hundred), *D* (five hundred), *M* (one thousand).

Voice:

Writers use numbers to count things. For numbers that consist of two words or fewer and for fractions (*twenty-six, eight, one-fifth*), writers most often use words. For longer numbers (*456; 8,343*), you will see figures. When numbers are very high (over a million), you will see a combination of words and figures (*11 million*). Of course, in technical or mathematical environments, figures are used almost exclusively. Numbers at the beginning of a sentence are spelled out with words.

Range/Habitat: In general, you will spot numbers as figures in these non-technical habitats: times of day, addresses; dates; exact amounts of money; decimals and fractions; percentages, scores and statistics; chapters, pages, scenes, and lines; and abbreviations. If percentages and money are fewer than four words (*50%, $38*), you will most often see words (*fifty percent, thirty-eight dinras*); otherwise, figures are used. In most writing, the numbers below 10 (ten) are written out as words, as are numbers in their plural form (thousands, millions).

After plural numbers, the singular form, *hundred, thousand,* and *million,* and *trillion* is used (*twelve hundred, 20 million,* for example). For the plural form of figures, the figure is often accompanied by an *s* (*the 1900s*). Arabic numbers have a global distribution and, while in the past they migrated, they are fairly stable in their present locations today. You will find Roman numerals in for-the-ages environments, such as on the cornerstones of buildings or, sometimes, in the printing dates of tomes as these numerals are very formal. Roman numerals are an endangered species and may, in the next fifty or so years, become extinct.

Examples: *One thousand fourteen workers escaped from the manufactory.*

Hundreds of bees enveloped her.

The war cost taxpayers over $1.7 trillion.

Established: MCMXXVI (1926)

Ninety percent of the fields were planted with corn.

A family of owls can kill and eat over three thousand rodents in a nesting season.

The ruins were of a city built in 5 B.C.E.

The oak tree was 20 m tall.

I believe it was some time in the 1980s when the exclamation mark on my sign disappeared.

Had-Had, the rat in the manufactory, was elderly; he was in his nineties.

The Number Sign

CLASS: Narratopsida
ORDER: Scriberales
FAMILY: Ligaturidae
GENUS: *Clathra*
SPECIES: *C. nota*

COMMON NAMES: Number Symbol, Pound Sign, Pound Symbol, Hash, Hashtag, Hash Mark, Hatch Mark, Octothorpe, Square (British)

Ancestral Record/ Pedigree:

One theory about the origins of this mark refers to old methods of weighing things as the pound sign meant: "pounds in the balance." The Latin term *libra pondo* meant exactly this. We today still use "lbs." as an abbreviation in writing for pounds even though the *libra* part translates as "balances" or "scales" and not *pondo*. The spoken term, "pounds," comes from the translation of the *pondo* part, which came from the Latin verb *pendere*, "to weigh." Eventually, in the fourteenth century, the "lb." as a shorthand for *libra* became an English unit of weight. Over the years, with writers and merchants adding a tilde mark (~) to connect the two letters, a typographic ligature (combination of two [or sometimes three] characters into a single one) was born, making this number sign look more as it does today.

Description/ Field Marks:	**The number sign consists of two sets of parallel lines:** **two vertical and two horizontal, overlapping.** Don't confuse this mark with the musical symbol called a sharp. While in both marks there are two pairs of parallel lines, the number sign has two horizontal lines while the sharp sign consists of two slanted lines, rising from left to right in order to avoid their being obscured on the horizontal lines of a musical staff.
Voice:	This mark is used to denote the word "number" (similar to *No.*) or to denote pounds, the weight of something in pounds *avoirdupois*. Just as *Amaranthus caudatus* has different names in different parts of the world (velvet flower, tassel flower, foxtail amaranth) so, too, does the number sign have names that vary from place to place. When it is found preceding numbers, it is called the number sign; on a telephone keypad, however, it is called "pound" or "the pound key."
Range/Habitat:	When you come across this mark before a number, it should be read as "number." For example, a #2 pencil is pronounced "a number two pencil." You might also find this mark *following* a number. In this case, it describes weight.
Examples:	*A #2 pencil can write effectively in zero gravity, upside down, and underwater.*

The importers ordered 1,200# of yams, which—being ipomoca batatas—*should have been marked as 1,200# of sweet potatoes.*

It is estimated that the burning of 3.78 L of gasoline, which weighs 2.83 kg, puts approximately 9.07 kg of GHG into the atmosphere.

Now contrast this with:

It is estimated that the burning of one gallon of gasoline, which weighs 6.25#, puts approximately 20# of GHG into the atmosphere.

Comments: Be aware that the range of this mark is changing. It is now commonly seen frequenting computers and various computer programs. When used with some computer applications, this mark is called a hash (or a hashtag).

Parentheses

CLASS: Narratopsida
ORDER: Scriberales
FAMILY: Interpunctidae
GENUS: *Amplecti*
SPECIES: *A. augmen*

COMMON NAMES: Parens (colloquial), Round Brackets

Ancestral Record/ Pedigree:

Parentheses evolved from similar symbols first documented in the late 14th century. These earlier forms were used by scribes and looked a bit like angle brackets (< >) in 1399. These paired symbols were used in an Italian 1428 printing of Cicero's *Epistolae ad familares.* Subsequently, the marks became more rounded (( )). Gaparino Barzizza (1359-1431) described the rounded form in his *Doctrina punctandi.* The name changed, also, from *virgulae convexae* to the coinage of *lunula* by Desiderius Erasmus (1466-1536) because the marks resembled the round shape of the moon. By the end of the 16th century, the term, *parenthesis*, (from the Latin for "insert beside") constituted a new name change, and the marks took on their current form and role.

Description/ Field Marks:

The parentheses consist of two arcs, the left (open or opening) parenthesis, and the right (close or closing) parenthesis. Between them, they enclose "parenthetical material"—material that serves to clarify or is an aside to the main point of text.

Voice: Writers often use parentheses in formal writing to add supplementary information (material that is of minor importance or secondary importance) and clarify, comment on, or illustrate what comes before it. The material inside the parentheses must not be grammatically integral to the surrounding sentence. Also, parentheses are needed as shorthand for an option of either singular or plural nouns.

Range/Habitat: You will often find parentheses embracing the area code of a telephone number, embracing a time zone, embracing the year of birth and death of a person, and embracing short unquoted text (in quoted text, brackets are more often found for translations). Parentheses may be nested inside of another set of parentheses. Any punctuation inside of parentheses is independent of the rest of the text. Another common habitat for parentheses is curved around numbers or letters in a list or curved around (enclosing) textual citations. Like brackets and quotation marks, parentheses traditionally mated for life, so if you saw one you could, with confidence, expect to spot another nearby. However, while one could expect to see two parentheses together in the past, a solitary parenthesis can more and more be observed today. Perhaps this is due to unequal birthrates; there appear to be more closing parens than opening ones. Another theory for the inequality is the exercise of greater independence in both types. It has been suggested by some researchers that opening parentheses might be more elusive than the closing ones. Yet another theory posits that there are external pressures on the population. It could also be that there are simply un-paired parentheses running around in a desperate search for mates. In any case, a function of our modern age, with its computer typing and emoticons, seems to have a bearing on the prevalence of a solitary parenthesis going about in the company of other marks, such as colons, hyphens, and commas.

There are traditional situations requiring ordered lists where you will see an unpaired closing parenthesis following a lowercase letter or a number. These solitary parentheses are usually found or used in educational testing, technical writing and diagrams, market research, and elections.

Examples: *Darla (a skunk,* Mephitis mephitis*) led Arden to the encampment.*

The Overseer refused to listen to the complaint(s).

Knave Psyllenquay (Was that his real name?) piloted a most unusual ship.

If you want to have your order expedited, you will need to submit the following items: (1) the order form, (2) a check for the total amount of the order, and (3) the completed return address label.

If you have any questions, please call me at (516) 555-6007.

The revolution will be televised at 6:00 p.m. (EST).

Divalion (1822-1905) had a long career as an opera singer; his clear tenor voice impressed all who heard it.

Her father told her about the Arabic رفـص *(zero) and how important it was.*

The spiders spun their thread (it was very strong, more like steel than thread), and she restrung her pearls on it.

The van driver was late again (why this should have surprised me, I don't know) and rushed around, causing me to forget to impart some important information (at least this is the reason [or excuse] that I came up with later).

I do not believe that good writing can be accomplished without clarity of both thought and execution, the latter through the use of proper punctuation. (But perhaps I am mistaken in my belief that people want to write well.)

After she picked up the coins from the path (something there was no reason not to do), she was surprised to learn that someone had deliberately placed them there.

The chirping sound of crickets is created by their running the top of one wing along the teeth at the bottom of the other wing. As a male cricket does this, he also holds the wings up and open so that the wing membranes can act as acoustical sails or amplifiers. This is called stridulation. Many people have the erroneous belief that the cricket chirps by rubbing its legs together (Randolph, 2007).

The dragline strength of spider silk is 1.3 GPa (a unit of measuring force per unit area); the strength of steel ranges from 0.2 GPa to nearly 2 GPa.

The Percent Sign

CLASS:	Narratopsida
ORDER:	Scriberales
FAMILY:	Enumeratidae
GENUS:	*Fragmen*
SPECIES:	*F. nota*

Ancestral Record/ Pedigree: Contrary to what one might believe, the two *o*'s or zeros of the percent sign did not evolve from the number 100. Research shows that in the 15th century, writers created a ligature, or picture, from the letters *p-c-o*, short for *per cento*, or "per hundred." The word, *per*, now a *p* instead of a word, collapsed under the *c*, which was now a closed circle topped by a horizontal line. On top of that was the *o* of *cento*. The *pc* with a loop turned into a horizontal fraction sign by 1650. The evolution of the percent sign was complete after the *per* vanished and the horizontal line became diagonal, a change that occurred during the 19th century.

Description/ Field Marks: **The percent sign is a diagonal slash with two small circles on either side of it.** It floats at the top of the line and usually follows a number of less than 100. However, if the number is written out as a word, you should see the word, "percent," and not the mark.

Voice: Writers use the percent sign to get across the idea of "parts per hundred." Newspapers and magazines usually use numerals (numbers) and the percent sign in order to save space. Because of its space-saving qualities, the percent sign is also richly represented in advertisements and store signs.

Range/Habitat: In titles and headings, writers usually write percent out as a word, so you will rarely spot the percent sign in these locations.

Examples: *Fourteen percent of the adult population, or over 32 million people, can't read.*

The number of non-readers is 14% of the general population, or over 32 million adults.

Over 70% of the world is covered by water, but only 2.5% of it is fresh (non-saline). Of that amount, just 1% is easily accessible. Over 68% of the fresh water is locked up in ice and glaciers. Another 30% is in the ground.

This Weekend Only! 50% off all linens!

The Period

CLASS: Narratopsida
ORDER: Scriberales
FAMILY: Interpunctidae
GENUS: *Clausula*
SPECIES: *C. ultimus*

COMMON NAMES: Period, Full Stop (British English), Aristophanes's Dot

Ancestral Record/ Pedigree:	The period evolved from one of the three dots that Aristophanes, a scholar and the chief of staff at the library of Alexandria, used in the 3rd century B.C.E to annotate the library's Greek scrolls. The precursor of our modern period was his high dot, which signaled the end of a sentence. Isidore of Seville (in what is now Spain) updated the dots of Aristophanes to match meaning and grammar instead of the pauses of oratory reading. Over the years, this system evolved yet more, with the period dropping to the bottom of the line.
Description/ Field Marks:	**This little creature is ubiquitous and rife, just as I am redundant! It is a small, round circle about the size of a pen or pencil dot.** While usually black, variations can be found in every color of the spectrum; it simply depends on what color ink is available.
Voice:	Periods are in the world primarily to designate endings of statements (or declarative sentences). Periods

also designate abbreviations. They show an end of things or a shortening of things.

Range/Habitat: The end of a sentence is most commonly home to the period. This mark is found lurking low, on the line or just ever so slightly above it. If a group of words has a subject and a verb without a subordinating conjunction (subordinator) in front of it, one should see a period at the end of it. Immediately after this kind of period, one will find a capital letter—the beginning of a new statement or of a question. Capitals are always found following a period. You will also find a period at the end of an imperative sentence—one that gives directions or a command and has a hidden subject of "you." In addition to ending statements, periods are prevalent in the area of abbreviations and in acronyms (though in the latter, they are often no longer found). If a sentence ends with a period marking an abbreviation, you should not see a second period.

Examples: *In many species of owls, one ear is higher than the other. This allows the owl to better determine the location of prey.*

An angry mob chased her across fields and into an orchard.

Ms. Griffin used to sell apples.

Don't climb a ladder unsupervised.

I asked her how old she was.

It was 4:00 a.m. Clearly, he had to be careful not to rouse the neighbors by making noise or turning on the lights.

The colors of a flame can indicate temperature. A dull red shows the area of 500-600 degrees C. Bright yellow shows 1200-1400 degrees C. White heat is in the 1400-1600 degree range.

Wild boars can reach up to 200 kg (440 lbs.), occasionally even 300 kg (661 lbs.). If surprised or cornered, they may become aggressive and can cause injury with their tusks. However, this is quite rare and usually only occurs when a sow feels protective of her piglets.

The Question Mark

CLASS:	Narratopsida
ORDER:	Scriberales
FAMILY:	Interpunctidae
GENUS:	*Clausula*
SPECIES:	*C. indagatio*

Ancestral Record/ Pedigree:	Some paleo-graphologists believe that the question mark evolved from a "lightning bolt" symbol discovered in the 8th century by Alcuin of York. A combination of a period and the lightning bolt (our modern tilde ~ is closest in resemblance) became the standard practice for punctuating questions and may have evolved into our modern mark. Alcuin named it *punctus interrogativus* and used it to denote a rising, questioning tone of voice. It came at the end of a question.
	Much later, when scholars in Paris standardized punctuation, they selected Alcuin's *punctus interrogativus* to carry the sole grammatical meaning of a question. The lightning bolt rotated into a more vertical position and so, with the dot below it, looked very much like the modern mark.
	However, other scholars have speculated that the question mark arose from Medieval Latin, when the word *quaestio* was truncated to a capital *q* written over the *o* and forming one letter (a ligature) to show "question."

Another researcher believes he found the earliest ancestor of the modern question mark in a 6th century Syriac manuscript. The mark may have functioned like an interrogative (questioning) notation, but with its double dots called *zagwa elaya*, it had the appearance of a modern colon.

Other theories border on the ridiculous, as is the one that purports a drawing of an Egyptian cat's tail to be the source of the modern mark. Clearly, the lineage of our curved line-atop-a-dot is still in dispute.

Description/ Field Marks:	**The question mark, like the exclamation point, is one of the tallest of the punctuation marks. At its very bottom is a noticeable point or dot, which looks like a period. Above this period is a curved hook, with its opening facing left.** One could say it resembles a cup hook or the very top of a shepherd's crook, or the sawn-off top of a cane. If it has a curved hook, it is this species.
Voice:	Writers use this mark to indicate a direct question. Question marks are never to be seen at the end of indirect questions, which report rather than ask. Do not waste your time looking for them there.
Range/Habitat:	The interrogative, or question, is home to this mark. It inhabits any areas where the need or desire to know is a constant.
Examples:	*How can a liter of gasoline, which weighs .75 kg, create 2.3 kg of greenhouse gas?*
	How can a gallon of gasoline, which weighs six and a quarter pounds, create twenty pounds of greenhouse gas?
	Is it true that the largest living organism in the world is not the blue whale but a fungus more than 10 square kilometers (4 square miles) in size?

"How far is it from here to Inkh?" she asked.

Comments: Note that in reported speech, you will not see
question marks.

She asked me how far it was from my vivarium to Inkh.

Quotation Mark

CLASS:	Narratopsida
ORDER:	Scriberales
FAMILY:	Interpunctidae
GENUS:	*Amplecti*
SPECIES:	*A. vox*

Ancestral Record/ Pedigree:

Today's quotation marks are the descendants of the 2nd century B.C. *diple*, first discovered and used by Aristarchus, a Greek-speaking librarian and the successor of Aristophanes at the noted institution at Alexandria. He added the *diple*, or "double" (>), an arrowhead shape in the margins of writings, to mark noteworthy lines. A few centuries later, writers used the *diple* to note quotations in religious texts. The *diple* changed in form, with the addition of a dot inside the *V* and with the *V*-shaped mark rotated. After the advent of the printing press, the *diple*, for some reason, fell out of fashion as type designers replaced it with double commas (,,) at the bottom of the line in the margins of cited examples of text. These double commas, later elevated to the top of the line, are more recent ancestors of our quotation marks. Claims regarding the discovery of these marks in history are difficult to verify. One claim is that Mathias Schurer, of Strasbourg, Alsace, discovered the marks. In 1516, he printed Flavius Philostratus's book, *De Vitis Sophistarum* wherein the *indicia* (marks) were placed in the lefthand margin of the lines where quoted material appeared. Another claim of the heritage of quotation marks is a 1555 French edition of Petrus Ramus's *Dialecticae partitiones*, published in Paris by Andre Wechel. The double quotation mark is older than the single, which emerged around 1800 to indicate a "quote within a quote," or secondary level of quotation.

Description/ Field Marks:	**There are two kinds of quotation marks, the opening and the closing, and they almost always are seen in one another's company because of their mating habits.** Be alert, however, as from a distance—especially in their single form—quotation marks can easily be confused with apostrophes. Apostrophes, however, are single strokes and almost always gad about alone. If you remember that quotation marks almost always travel as a pair, you should not have any difficulty distinguishing this species from apostrophes.
Voice:	Writers use quotation marks to surround a direct quote—the exact words that someone said or wrote which the writer is repeating. They can also surround a single word or phrase to express sarcasm, irony, or skepticism. Writers express this on paper, but speakers very often do this in the air with their hands. When speakers use quotation marks in this way, they will make a gesture with two fingers on each hand, curling once or twice to "draw" the quotation marks. This motion, if not understood as gestural quotes, is unintelligible to many people. Gestural quotation marks are used to mean "so-called." Some people refer to them as "air quotes." Quotation marks may be used to set off words. Another use of of them is to enclose the title of a short or subsidiary work, like a story in an anthology, a chapter, or an episode. If quotation marks are used inside another pair of quotation marks, the double quotes surround the primary quoted material and the embedded secondary quoted material is enclosed by single quote marks (which look like apostrophes). The

only environment in which you might find the double closing quotation mark without its mate is to denote the measurement of inches (the single closing quotation mark [or the apostrophe] is used in this same way as an abbreviation for feet).

Range/Habitat: You can find quotation marks enclosing the exact words that someone said, thought, or wrote. The opening mark will almost always be found immediately to the left of a capital letter. The closing mark will be after a period, exclamation point, question mark, or (less frequently) a comma. In addition, look for these marks at the beginning and end of the title of a short work or surrounding a "word as a word" or an ironic word or phrase.

Examples: *Arden said, "The mourning dove told me, 'If I go there alone, I'll be eaten alive and then spit up,' so I couldn't not help."*

Her shard knife was about 8" long.

Her shard knife was about 20 cm long.

The "vine-ripened" tomatoes very obviously had been gassed with ethylene after being picked green.

"How far is it from here to Inkh?" she asked.

The question is: "What are we busy about?"

Dr. Dayao Lenatkis observes that the $15 billion agriculture business will collapse significantly if "neonicotinoid pesticides are not banned."

"I'm feeling very sick!" Dolcezza said.

Nash Oppozinolitelli comments that "anxiety over this state of affairs is completely unfounded."

The word, shampoo, comes from Sanskrit via Hindi and

means "to knead" or "to soothe."

In Vida Malaya's short story, "Ishma Gozal," the main character is a prescient goatherd.

Comments: You should not see quotation marks with indirect or reported speech. If you do, call Fish and Wildlife or Animal Control right away.

One boy interviewed by this researcher said that he had never seen a a real butterfly—only some on decals and stickers, in advertising logos, on T.V., and in some virtual games.

As Exotics: *One boy interviewed by this researcher said, "that he had never seen a a real butterfly—only some on decals and stickers, in advertising logos, on T.V., and in some virtual games."*

She asked me "how far it was from here to Inkh."

The Semicolon

CLASS:	Narratopsida
ORDER:	Scriberales
FAMILY:	Interpunctidae
GENUS:	*Clausula*
SPECIES:	*C. pausa*

Ancestral Record/ Pedigree:
Aldus Manutius, of italics fame [see Italics], is credited with having used the very first semicolon in the early 1500s.

Description/ Field Marks:
The semicolon looks like a cross between a comma and a period, with the comma situated directly under an elevated period.

Voice:
Writers use the semicolon when they want to signal closely related clauses. A semicolon is stronger than a comma and weaker than a period. The clause after the semicolon expands on or contrasts with the clause before the semicolon. Often, the semicolon introduces a restatement of the idea in the first clause. It can also separate elements in a list when each element of the list is long and complex.

Range/Habitat:
Semicolons are very often followed by an independent clause. They inhabit the space between two independent clauses where the second one is headed by a transition (transitional expression or conjunctive adverb), such as *however*, *therefore*, *in fact*, *consequently*, *finally*, *on the*

contrary, then, moreover. However, another location might be in front of *for example, namely,* or *that is* with a series of phrases. Semicolons seem to like series or lists, but they do not usually begin them. That is the domain of colons. When a series (list) includes elements that already contain internal commas, you should see each element of the list separated by a semicolon. In quotations, you will see the semicolon outside the closing quotation mark. This is also true for single closing quotation marks.

Examples:

The owls debated every statement; they believed oppositional thinking helped uncover what was true.

There were only a handful of subjects that the Reigning Cats permitted to be taught in the schools; for example, Roaming, Ravaging, and Regurgitating.

Wild boars eat all kinds of plants; moreover, they eat insects and small rodents.

To spin their webs, most spiders have the ability to produce three, or more, different kinds of silk: an elastic one, which can stretch like a rubber band; a strong one, which can be stronger than steel on a per-weight basis; and a sticky or adhesive one.

Tomorrow, I need to do several maintenance tasks: remove the Apostrophes from their tank; scrub the inside glass of the tank with distilled white vinegar; rinse and thoroughly dry the glass; refill the tank with fresh water; and, finally, return all the Apostrophes to it.

The people on the shore waited for the Aviso to dock; then, they rejoiced.

Mr. Psyllenquay said, "I will give you direction"; it was a misleading statement.

The Slash

CLASS: Narratopsida
ORDER: Scriberales
FAMILY: Interpunctidae
GENUS: *Ecfio*
SPECIES: *E. optio*

COMMON NAMES: The Diagonal, The Bar, The Virgule, The *Solidus*, The Stroke (Brit. English), The Forward Slash

Ancestral Record/ Pedigree:

Evidence of an early relationship between the slash and the virgule (Latin for "twig") has been widely found. The latter for a long time functioned as what today we call the comma, dash, period, and caesura. All denote pauses in recitation (or singing) of text. In the 12th century, the Italian writer Boncompagno da Signa created a punctuation system which used only two marks: a slash (/) and a dash (—). The slash denoted a pause (*virgula suspensiva*), and the dash ended a sentence. In some locations, the slash continued to serve this purpose even as the comma migrated into the position of showing a pause. The slash was also used to mark the continuation of a word onto the next line of a page. This usage was later replaced by the hyphen. In 18th century England, the slash mark was renamed the "oblique," a name it held until a reclassification changed the name to "stroke." The appellation of "slash" is of recent coinage from American English around 1961.

This name is now the most widely used when the mark is used in the context of computing.

Description/ Field Marks:	**The slash is a line, tilted toward the right, from the bottom to the top.** At a distance, a slash can be confused with a solidus (which is more tilted and, consequently, longer) or the fraction slash in mathematics, which is used to separate the top numerator from the bottom denominator for division operations, ratios, and fractions. Environment and context will give you a clue as to which one you are viewing or which one you want to use.
Voice:	Writers use the slash to separate choices or alternatives. A slash can sometimes be seen used as shorthand for an "exclusive *or*" (e.g. Y/N, pass/fail, and/or). Slashes are also a good way to mark divisions between two or three lines of poetry quoted in a text. They separate paired items, such as singer/songwriter, and are found in internet addresses and in some abbreviations.
Range/Habitat:	This is one of the rarest marks in formal writing though it can be found there when the habitat contains poetry. In this case, you will see a space on either side of the slash. This indicates a line break in the original poem. However, more than three lines of poetry should be handled as an indented quotation.
	Some of the more informal habitats that are good locations for viewing the slash include when it serves as shorthand for *per*; when it is expressing the idea of "or"; when it is expressing the idea of "and"; when it indicates that something spans two years; when it represents a conflict or connection between two things; when it functions as a stand-in for the Latin, *cum*, which means "combined with," "along with being," or "also used as." Often, you will see the slash in certain common abbreviations, in fractions, and in informal dates.

Examples: *She needed a cord 1/2 the original length.*

Everyone must present his/her ticket before entering the museum.

When a new leader is elected, he/she will have a lot of work to do in reuniting a fractious population.

When a new leader is elected, s/he will have a lot of work to do in reuniting a fractious population.

In the play, "Gravity of the Moon," the character of Delia ends her poem with, "Tides rise and fall, / Its influence is of no small consequence / As it delicately throws a curve on falling bodies."

He was more comfortable and skilled in teaching Music Theory/Musical Composition than the prescribed courses demanded by the new regime.

For more information, go to http://www.info.gov.

The local butcher offered to pay her $3.00/hr.

A honeybee can fly 24-32 km/h.

One wonders whether the nurture/nature debate will ever be resolved.

The hurricanes of 2005/06 numbered 38, the most in recorded history.

She constructed a bower-cum-bedroom.

She constructed a bower/bedroom.

c/o (in care of)

w/ (with)

w/out or *w/o* (without)

He wrote the check on 7/21/05.

O

The Space

CLASS: Narratopsida
ORDER: Scriberales
FAMILY: Interpunctidae
GENUS: *Spatium*
SPECIES: *S. plurimus*

Ancestral Record/ The space has always existed but has not always
Pedigree: been utilized.

Description/ **A space is a blank area devoid of content. It serves to**
Field Marks: **separate words, letters, numbers, and punctuation. This**
mark is noticed more for its absence than its presence.
There are two major kinds of space marks: the *em* space
and the *en* space. The former is the width of the letter *M*,
and the latter is as wide as the letter *N* or, more technically
now, half the width of the *em* space. If you don't see
anything, then what you are looking at is this species.

Voice: Spaces give a reader visual clues as to where
one word ends and another begins on a page.
Just as the development of Aristophanes's system of
dots created greater ease for reading because
EVERYWORDWASNOTCROWDED, the
employment of spaces has increased reading efficiency.

Range/Habitat: The space follows each word in a text in a way similar
to how remora fish follow sharks. A single space is

always present after a period. In former years, two spaces would attach themselves to the end of a sentence after each period, but today you will spot only a single one.

Example: *Any sentence at all will give ample evidence supportive of the existence and necessity of the space.*

The Underline

CLASS:	Narratopsida
ORDER:	Scriberales
FAMILY:	Graphidae
GENUS:	*Funis*
SPECIES:	*F. gravis-subpositio*

Description/ Field Marks:	**The underline is a horizontal line written under a word, a space, or a line of text.**
Voice:	Writers use underlines to set words or phrases apart. They give emphasis, mimicking what is called stress in spoken language. The underline is closely related to italics and is regarded now as a subspecies of *I. gravis*. [See Italics]. In handwritten text, writers use the underline wherever italics would appear in type.
Range/Habitat:	The underline is a rarity these days, so consider yourself very lucky if you should spot one. Its ecological niche has been almost completely supplanted by italics. I cannot even remember the last time someone ordered an underline from my vivarium and, in consequence, am hard-pressed to justify my continuing to raise them. Occasionally, if you look very carefully in an email address (URL), you can find one but, because of the dearth of handwritten texts these days (keyboarding being so popular), it's possible that the underline is on its way to extinction. Perhaps one day

in the future, we will only be able to see an underline in a zoo.

Examples: *Lucy Bosphorus <lg_bosphorus@exq.com>*

They knocked on the door for five minutes, but no one opened it though they were aware that someone was inside.

Do not attempt this at home.

Afterword

The purpose of punctuation is to make things clear, to ease readers along in their understanding, to express what writers have in mind. While I am coming to understand that new, computer/digital conventions are arising, we must judge them by the criteria of clarity, ease, and expression. Speed or brevity in writing, or mere cleverness, is not a strong enough justification for dispensing with clarity.

I was recently sent copies of the following by a friend. She had received them as emails. I will be quick to admit that I am a bit old-fashioned, but I would imagine most readers would stumble quite as much as I did when reading these two communications for the first time. To wit:

Ey Cuzns & Bro,

M makin plnz 4 Nov n 1dering f Fri, 27th, w%d wrk 4 U 2 gt 2gtha. NE1 bz or outa twn dat dy?

Hope ll S wel~

Luv,
June

Evry1, really appreci8 d spED repllz. Alan, thx so mch 4 offrin 2 mEt @ ur house. Wl B a gr8t tym! L%kin fwd 2 CN U ll.

WishN U holidA cheer =)
June

If this kind of writing were to catch on and become the norm, it would certainly be good for my business—all those new ways to use punctuation marks! My sales of percent signs, numbers, capital letters, and parentheses would skyrocket.

But the question is whether clarity is sacrificed. If so, no amount of monetary gain—for me or anyone—can counteract the bad idea that such muddle represents.

If you are tempted to defy the tested, clarifying benefits of punctuation as have been offered in this field guide and to mimic these two examples above, please first ask yourself, before applying pen to paper or fingers to keys: "At what cost?"

Let us not sacrifice our thoughts, our thinking, our readers' engagement, or our communication with others to the demands of new technologies for the sake of those technologies, nor to misguided innovation or self-indulgent individuality. Let us not jeopardize or fracture our community.

Glossary

Adjectives: see Parts of Speech

Adverbs: see Parts of Speech

Appositives: An appositive is a noun that follows another noun and renames or gives additional information to the first one. Because the appositive or second noun is extra information, it is set off with commas (if it is in the middle of the sentence) or with one comma (if it is at the end of the sentence).

EX: *Her brother, Oliver, was angry that she borrowed his things.*

       Oliver, her brother, was angry that she borrowed his things.

       There were two helpful people in Onley, a farming community not too far from the vivarium.

Auxiliary Verbs: see Helping Verbs

Clauses: A clause is a subject and its verb. There are many different kinds of clauses in English.

Independent

The most common clause is an independent one, which can stand by itself in a sentence and express a complete meaning. An independent clause is also called the main clause.

EX: *The apples were ripe.*

                Nicker bean bushes tore her jacket.

                Acorns become oak trees.

                I am a scientist.

                It rained.

Dependent

There are three main kinds of dependent (relative) clauses: Subordinate, Adjective, and Noun.

Subordinate

One kind of clause is a subordinate clause—one that is less important than an independent clause and doesn't express a complete idea. It is headed by a subordinator [see Joining Words]. This kind of dependent clause can follow the independent clause, in which case there is no comma. If the dependent clause comes before the independent clause, there should be a comma before the main subject of the independent clause.

Adjective

An adjective clause comes immediately after the noun that it describes. There are two kinds of adjective clauses and they require different punctuation.

Non-restrictive (Non-identifying, Non-defining)

A non-restrictive adjective clause gives extra information about a noun that has already been identified in some way.

This kind of adjective clause cannot be headed by the word, "that." It can only be headed by these relative pronouns:

who (for people or anthropomorphized animals [with names] who are in the subject position)

whom (for people or anthropomorphized animals [with names] in the object position)

which (for non-people, things)

whose (for possessive nouns)

where (for places or locations)

when (for times)

EX:

*Knave, **who operated a strange paddlewheel boat**, condemned her as she ran up the gangplank.*

*The moon, **which makes a complete orbit around Earth in approximately 28 days**, has an important effect on the tides of the ocean.*

*Arden, **whom he had been following for days**, continued to evade him.*

*Dander Industries, **which orders many different punctuation marks from me**, is a well-known exporter.*

*Fat Cat, **whose takeover caused the imprisonment of thousands of Dogs**, did not believe music education was important.*

*Arden wanted to get back to Ankh, **where her family and friends lived**.*

*By that afternoon, **when the van driver finally showed up**, I had already fixed my sign.*

Restrictive (Identifying, Defining)

A restrictive adjective clause limits the noun. It answers the question: "Which one?" There is no comma between it and the noun it describes because it is not extra information. It is essential information for identifying the noun. In a restrictive adjective clause, the relative pronouns can be the same as for non-restrictive. However, with the exceptions of "whose," "when," and "where," the relative pronoun should be "that." When "whom," "which," or "that" are objects of the adjective clause, the relative pronoun can be dropped completely.

EX: *The man **who/that operated a strange paddlewheel boat** condemned her as she ran up the gangplank.*

*The planetary body **which/that makes a complete orbit around Earth in approximately 28 days** is the moon.*

*The small round object **that/which/ø the wild boar sow rooted up** was a pearl.*

*The girl **whom/that/ø he had been following for days** continued to evade him.*

*The company **which/that orders many different punctuation marks from me** is a well-known exporter.*

*The leader **whose takeover caused the imprisonment of thousands of Dogs** did not believe music education was important.*

*Arden wanted to get back to the town **where her family and friends lived**.*

*This coming Thursday at noon is the only time **when I can meet you**.*

Noun

A noun clause is commonly the object of the verb. More rarely (and in more formal writing), it can be the subject in an independent clause. Noun clauses are very often used for reported/indirect speech. They can be headed with the word, "that," if they are in the object position, but this is optional and more formal. If they are headed with a question word, they are embedded questions [see Indirect Speech]. Many times, a noun clause follows the verbs: " said," "think," "feel," "sense," "believe," "know," and "see." Other verbs, such as "counter," "assume," "state," "argue," "posit" (and others), are also often followed by a noun clause.

EX: *The cricket said [SOMETHING].*
        The cricket said (that) he would taste the puffballs.

        I believe [SOMETHING].
        I believe (that) punctuation is important.

        [SOMETHING] greatly concerns me.
        That faulty punctuation obscures meaning greatly concerns me.

        It greatly concerns me that faulty punctuation obscures meaning.

To find a noun clause, it is helpful to ask the question, "What?" In the above examples, what did the cricket say? What do I believe? What greatly concerns me?

Comma Faults/Comma Splices: This occurs when two independent clauses are "joined" by a comma only and the necessary coordinator (joining word) is missing. A comma can not join two independent clauses [see Joining Words] unless they are in a series or list of more than two independent clauses.

EX: *Puffballs are known styptics, they can contract tissue to seal up injured blood vessels and stop bleeding.* [incorrect]

Complex Sentences: A complex sentence is one with a main, independent clause and a dependent (subordinate) clause [see Clauses and Joining Words].

Compound Adjectives: A compound adjective is a single adjective consisting of more than one word. It often contains a hyphen, which shows that the multiple words are part of the same adjective.

EX: *well-known*
              a twin-engine plane
              a 20-page document
              She was a 10-year-old girl.

Compound Nouns: A compound noun is a noun consisting of two or more words. Most are made with nouns which are described by other nouns. In other words, the first noun is acting like an adjective for the second noun. Sometimes these two nouns are open or spaced compounds (written as separate words), sometimes they are closed or solid compounds (written as single words), and sometimes they are hyphenated compounds (connected with a hyphen). Check a good dictionary.

	OPEN	CLOSED	HYPHENATED
EX:	*bus stop*	*toothpaste*	*sister-in-law*
	fire sale	*mailbox*	*boar-sow*
	swimming pool	*grasshopper*	*ice-ax*

Other compound nouns consist of an adjective and a noun.

EX: *full moon*   *redbird*

A compound noun might also consist of a noun and a verb.

EX: *sunrise*   *hairstyle*

Compound Sentences: A compound sentence is made up of two independent clauses that are joined with a coordinator (coordinating conjunction) [see Joining Words].

EX: *Puffballs are known* styptics, ***for*** *they can contract tissue to seal up injured blood vessels and stop bleeding.*

Conjunctions: see Joining Words

Conjunctive Adverbs: see Joining Words, Transitions

Contractions: The verb, "contract," means "become smaller or tighter." It is an antonym of the verb, "expand." Since the word is a verb and two syllables, the stress is on the second syllable. If you stress the first syllable, you have the noun, "contract," a legal written agreement between people or companies.

Contractions are ways to make sentences shorter, and they are fertile ground for apostrophes. Please note that the use of contractions makes writing less formal (or more informal). Some of the more common contractions are with the verb "be":

She is	*She's*	*They are*	*They're*
I am	*I'm*	*We are*	*We're*
There is	*There's*	*That is*	*That's*
You are	*You're*		

Contractions are also common with "will" to show future:

He will	*He'll*	*They will*	*They'll*
I will	*I'll*	*We will*	*We'll*
There will	*There'll*	*That will*	*That'll*
You will	*You'll*		

You will also see them for "have," "has," and "had," but only when these words are auxiliary/helping verbs (for perfect tenses). The verb "have" or "has" or "had" is not contracted. Also, we rarely contract "had" with the subject "it" as the pronunciation is rather difficult. In writing, the helping verbs "have," "has," and "had" are usually not contracted for proper nouns [see Parts of Speech: Noun]. In formal writing, "have," "has," and "had" as the helping verb are never contracted.

She's been walking for a long time.

They'd be better off planting a variety of crops.

Before I realized my mistake, the van had already gone.

Before I realized my mistake, the van'd already gone. [incorrect]

When you read *'d* (apostrophe *d*), be careful as this contraction is for both "had" and "would."

EX: *She'd like to find a ship to take her home.* (would)

          She'd never eaten oak cakes before. (had)

Dependent Clauses: see Clauses, Dependent

Direct Speech: When you read or write the exact words that a person says, this is direct or quoted speech. The direct speech is in quotation marks, and there is a comma separating the quote from the speakers (usually near "said," "told," or "asked") or inside the close quotation mark if the speaker comes after the quotation. Note that there isn't a comma if other punctuation ends the quote.

EX: *The skunk told her, "How you are feeling is controlling what you do."*

          "How you are feeling is controlling what you do," the skunk told her.

          The Overseer asked, "Can you sew?"

          "Can you sew?" asked the Overseer.

          "Can you sew?" the Overseer asked.

Embedded Questions: see Indirect Speech

Helping Verb: Helping verbs, sometimes called auxiliary verbs, help the main verb to express time, mood, or voice. The most common helping verbs are "do/does/did" for all verbs that are not "to be" (especially in question formation and negative statements); "have/has" plus the past participle of the verb for the present perfect tense; "had" plus the past participle for past perfect tense; and "am/is/are/was/were" plus the past participle for passive voice.

Independent Clauses: see Clauses

Indirect Speech: Indirect speech is also called reported speech because it reports what someone said. In formal writing and if quite a bit of time has elapsed between when the person said what he or she said and when you report it, there is a change of tense.

EX: *The skunk told her, "How you are feeling is controlling what you do."* [direct speech]

The skunk told her (that) how she was feeling was controlling what she did. [indirect speech]

She said, "I don't remember how to figure out how fast I can swim." [direct speech]

She said (that) she didn't remember how to figure out how fast she could swim. [indirect speech]

In the examples of indirect speech above, what was told or said is the object of the verb "told" or "said." The objects of these verbs are noun clauses.

When the indirect speech is reproducing a question, since the question is in the object position of the sentence, it needs to be in clause order. This simply means that the subject is first and the verb follows it. A change in the verb tense may also be necessary.

EX: *The reporter for the Newtamee Herald-Tribune asked me, "How much do you charge for each hyphen?"* [direct speech]

The reporter for the Newtamee Herald-Tribune asked me how much I charged for each hyphen. [indirect speech/embedded question]

As you can see from the above example, there is the WH-question word(s) ("how much") and then the subject ("I") and then the verb ("charged"). In indirect speech, a change of the pronouns is necessary.

If the direct speech/quoted speech question is a YES/NO question, the pattern is a little different. You will need to insert the word "if" or the word "whether" before the subject and verb."

EX: *"Have you ever swum across a river before?" asked the cricket.* [direct speech]

The cricket asked if she had ever swum across a river before. [indirect speech/embedded question]

The cricket asked whether she had ever swum across a river before. [indirect speech/embedded question]

Often, the words, "or not" are used in this situation. When using "whether," you can place the "or not" in two different locations. When using "if," you have only one option.

EX: *The cricket asked if she had ever swum across a river before or not.*

The cricket asked whether she had ever swum across a river before or not. [indirect speech/embedded question]

In both examples above, however, the "or not" at the end is so far away from the "if" or the "whether" that a reader will be surprised or confused by it. A better usage of the "or not" is immediately after "whether."

EX: *The cricket asked whether or not she had ever swum across a river before.*

Omit the "or not" when using "if" when the embedded question is quite long.

The cricket asked if she had ever swum across a river before. [indirect speech/embedded question]

The Overseer asked, "Can you sew?" [direct speech]

The Overseer asked if she could sew. [indirect speech]

The Overseer asked if she could sew or not. [indirect speech]

The Overseer asked whether she could sew. [indirect speech]

The Overseer asked whether she could sew or not. [indirect speech]

The Overseer asked whether or not she could sew. [indirect speech]

In indirect speech, there is no comma between the main verb and the report. This is a little different from the way some languages other than English behave. If you are not sure, ask yourself if this sentence makes sense:

I cleaned, the glass tanks.

We do not put a comma between a verb and its object [see Objects] unless some kind of extra information is inserted between them, in which case there will be at least two commas.

Introductory Phrases: see Phrases

Joining Words: Joining words, or conjunctions, most often connect independent clauses or other sentence elements. They show a relationship, or idea, that connects the clauses logically. There are three different kinds of joining words: coordinators (coordinating conjunctions); subordinators (subordinating conjunctions); and transition words (sometimes called signal words, transitional expressions, or conjunctive adverbs).

Coordinators

Coordinators join equal elements and express different ideas. There are seven coordinators in English, and a classic way to remember them is with the mnemonic, FANBOYS. This stands for the coordinators "for," "and," "nor," "but," "or," "yet", and "so." The coordinator "for" shows the idea of cause. The coordinator "and" shows the idea of addition. The coordinator "nor" expresses the idea of negative addition. The coordinator "but" shows the idea of difference or opposition. The coordinator "or" shows the idea of choice. The coordinator "yet" expresses the idea of contrast, and the coordinator "so" expresses the idea of result. In terms of frequency of use, however, a better mnemonic might be ABSO FYN. This can help you remember, also, that "or" and "nor" (the last letters of both menemonic parts) are often used as correlatives (two-part joining words).

When a coordinator joins two independent clauses, a comma comes before the coordinator. However, when a coordinator joins any other two equal elements, no comma is needed.

EX: *I am writing this field guide, for I believe an understanding of punctuation helps a person read or write better.*

There are seven coordinators in English, and they each express a different idea between two equal elements of a sentence.

He told me that he needed one gross of quotation marks and that he needed the order right away.

He told me that he needed one gross of quotation marks and needed the order right away.

He needed one gross of quotation marks, and he needed the order right away.

She was tired and hungry.

Correlative Coordinators

Notice that when you use the coordinator, "nor," it often is in a sentence with "neither." When "nor" alone joins two independent clauses, the word order of the second clause changes.

EX: *I am neither a prescriptivist nor a grammarian.*

The spiders neither scared her nor harmed her.

It is neither raining nor snowing today.

Some people will not listen to reasonable, opposing viewpoints, nor will they change their opinions.

Subordinators

Subordinators make a clause dependent, which means that it can not be alone in a sentence as it does not contain a complete idea. A dependent clause must be with an independent clause in a sentence [see Clauses, Dependent]. There should not be a comma preceding (coming before) a subordinator.

There are many subordinators, and they convey different ideas. Some of the subordinators show the idea of time:

before	*after*	*while*
since	*until*	*when*
as	*as soon as*	*whenever*
once	*by the time (that)*	*the moment (that)*

Some subordinators show the idea of condition:

if	*unless*

Some subordinators show the idea of cause (why?):

because	*since*	*as*
in that	*in as much as*	

Some subordinators show the idea of difference or opposition:

although	*even though*	*though*

Some subordinators show the idea of contrast:

whereas	*while*	*although*

Transitions

Transitions join the ideas of two independent clauses by introducing the second clause and showing an idea or relationship between them. You have two choices for punctuation. You can end the first independent clause with a period and start the second independent clause with a capitalized transition word and a comma before the main subject of the second clause, or you can end the first clause with a semicolon and write the transition word in lowercase with a comma before the main subject of the second independent clause.

EX:　　　　*She loved to eat. Therefore, she rooted around for acorns.*

　　　　　She loved to eat; therefore, she rooted around for acorns.

Of course, in the above example, because the idea between the clauses is one of result/reason or cause/effect, you could also join the two clauses with a coordinator or with a subordinator.

EX:　　　　*She loved to eat, so she rooted around for acorns.* (coordinator)

　　　　　She rooted around for acorns because she loved to eat.
　　　　　(subordinator heading its dependent clause)

　　　　　Because she loved to eat, she rooted around for acorns.
　　　　　(dependent clause before the independent clause)

There are many transitions, and they convey different ideas.

Some transitions show the idea of time:

then	*first*	*next*
later	*eventually*	*soon*
finally		

The most common transition shows the idea of difference or opposition:

　　　　however

Some transitions show the idea of contrast:

　　　　on the other hand　　*in contrast*

Some transitions show commentary:

　　　　unfortunately　　　*fortunately*

Some transitions show the idea of addition:

　　　　also　　　　　　　*in addition*　　　　*furthermore*

Some transitions show the idea of summary:

in other words   *in conclusion*   *in summary*

Main Clauses: see Clauses, Independent

Nouns: see Parts of Speech

Objects: The object of a sentence follows the verb and receives its action. English is a Subject-Verb-Object language.

Participles: The participle is a form of the verb.

Past Participle

When a verb is a regular verb, the past participle (or the "third form" of the verb) is very simple. It is exactly the same as the past simple tense form, made with "-ed."

EX:	base form	past simple	past participle
	walk	*walked*	*walked*

However, for irregular verbs, the past participle often looks very different from the past simple tense form:

EX:	base form	past simple	past participle
	go	*went*	*gone*

Some patterns for the past participle form of irregular verbs do emerge, however. One pattern contains *n* or *en*.

EX:	base form	past simple	past participle
	break	*broke*	*broken*
	choose	*chose*	*chosen*
	eat	*ate*	*eaten*

take	*took*	*taken*
write	*wrote*	*written*
draw	*drew*	*drawn*
know	*knew*	*known*
see	*saw*	*seen*

Present Participle

The present participle form of a verb is made by adding "-ing" to the base form (first form) of the verb. Most of the time, this is fairly straightforward. However, if the base form of the verb ends with a silent *e*, or if the word is one syllable ending with a consonant-vowel-consonant spelling combination, some additional thinking is involved. When there is a silent *e*, it gets dropped before adding the "-ing." With the consonant-vowel-consonant combination, the final consonant doubles before the addition of the "-ing."

EX:
walk	*walking*
ride	*riding*
run	*running*

The present participle form can be a verb (after a form of "be"), a noun (gerund), or an adjective.

EX: *She was helping me wrap packages when she looked out the window and saw a dangerous situation.* (past continuous/past progressive)

Helping others is a virtue. (gerund/noun)

What I needed was a helping hand. (adjective)

Parts of Speech:

Adverb
An adverb describes a verb, an adjective, or another adverb.

Adjective
An adjective describes a noun.

Noun
A noun is a person, place, thing, idea, or state. Proper nouns are named nouns. They begin with a capital letter.

Verb
A verb expresses an action or a state. It is the main part of a sentence. Verbs are the only part of speech to change for showing the time or tense. In statements, a verb follows the subject of the sentence.

Preposition
A preposition shows location, direction, or relationship.

Pronoun
A pronoun replaces a noun.

Passive Voice: Readers and listeners expect the subject of a sentence to be the performer, actor, or agent of the verb. If this is the case, a sentence is said to be in active voice. However, sometimes writers want to focus on the object of a sentence—because it is most important; because they don't know what or who performed the verb; because it's clear to everyone what or who performed the verb; or because they want to hide the performer and its agency.

When writers put the non-acting receiver of the verb (object) as the subject of the sentence, they need to signal this in some way. The tool for this is "to be" followed by the past participle (third form) of the verb. Sometimes, the "by phrase" is retained; sometimes, it is dropped.

EX: *The owl didn't eat the rat.* (active voice; focus is on the owl)

The rat wasn't eaten by the owl.
(passive voice; focus is on the rat)

The rat wasn't eaten.

Many buildings were damaged.

An important piece of my sign was stolen.

The scofflaw was arrested.

Many mistakes were made.

Phrases: A phrase is a group of words that does not have a subject with its verb. When a phrase comes before an independent clause, it is called an introductory phrase; there is a comma before the main subject of the independent clause [see Clauses, Independent].

Plural Nouns: Most plural nouns in English are made by adding an "-s" or an "-es".

EX:
noun	*nouns*
cataract	*cataracts*
river	*river*
van	*vans*
kiss	*kisses*
dish	*dishes*
lunch	*lunches*
box	*boxes*

However, there are quite a few irregular plural forms.

EX:
person	*people*
woman	*women*
man	*men*
fish	*fish*
sheep	*sheep*
child	*children*
foot	*feet*
goose	*geese*
louse	*lice*
mouse	*mice*
tooth	*teeth*

Many words that end with an *-o* are pluralized by adding *-es*.

EX:
echo	*echoes*
hero	*heroes*
potato	*potatoes*

tomato	*tomatoes*
tornado	*tornadoes*
torpedo	*torpedoes*

Many nouns that end with *-f* are pluralized by changing the *-f* to *-ves*.

EX:

calf	*calves*
elf	*elves*
half	*halves*
hoof	*hooves*
knife	*knives*
leaf	*leaves*
life	*lives*
loaf	*loaves*
self	*selves*
shelf	*shelves*
thief	*thieves*
wife	*wives*
wolf	*wolves*

Some plurals from Latin are even more confusing as they retain their Latinate form.

EX:

addendum	*addenda*
alumnus	*alumni*
antenna	*antennae*
bacterium	*bacteria*
cactus	*cacti*
cercus	*cerci*
curriculum	*curricula*
datum	*data*
genus	*genera*
medium	*media*
stimulus	*stimuli*
syllabus	*syllabi*
thesaurus	*thesauri*

Also from Latin are these irregular plurals, which change an *-ix* ending to an *-ices* one.

EX:

appendix	*appendices*
index	*indices*
matrix	*matrices*

Other irregular noun plurals (also from Latin) change a noun ending in -*is* to a plural form ending in -*es*.

EX:

axis	*axes*
analysis	*analyses*
basis	*bases*
crisis	*crises*
diagnosis	*diagnoses*
ellipsis	*ellipses*
emphasis	*emphases*
hypothesis	*hypotheses*
neurosis	*neuroses*
oasis	*oases*
paralysis	*paralyses*
parenthesis	*parentheses*

Possessive Nouns: Possessiveness shows ownership and this sense of ownership is conveyed with an apostrophe. Where people often get confused is when a plural noun is possessive. As a general rule, for plural nouns that do not end in -*s*, form the possessive by adding an apostrophe and -*s*. For plural nouns that end in -*s*, add only the apostrophe.

EX: *It was Oliver's book.*

The spider's silk was very strong. (one spider)

The spiders' silk was very strong. (two or more spiders)

The child's clothes were dirty. (one child)

The children's clothes were dirty. (children is an irregular plural)

She went into Mrs. Jones's fabric store.

Mr. and Mrs. Jones have a store on Main Street.
The Joneses have a store on Main Street. (plural; not possessive)

111

We are going to go to the Joneses' store after work. (plural, possessive)

It is a good idea to avoid writing inanimate nouns as possessive nouns because inanimate things cannot, technically, "own" anything.

EX: *The tree's bark was rough.*

             The bark of the tree was rough. (better)

             The table's leg was broken.

             The leg of the table was broken. (better)

This is a matter of style, however, and, often, an inanimate possessive noun may be unavoidable.

Possessive Pronouns: Also called possessive adjectives, these words replace possessive nouns. They must agree with the original noun in gender and in number. You will see them before a noun. However, sometimes other adjectives come between a possessive pronoun/adjective and the noun it describes.

EX: *It was Oliver's book.*
             It was his book.
             It was Oliver's battered, unread book.
             It was his battered, unread book.

             The book was Oliver's.
             The book was his.
             The battered, unread book was Oliver's.
             The battered, unread book was his.

             Everyone was surprised by the spiders' handiwork.
             Everyone was surprised by their handiwork.

The possessive adjectives:

             my
             his
             her
             your

our
their
its

Prepositions: see Parts of Speech

Pronouns: see Parts of Speech

Quoted Speech: see Direct Speech

Relative Clauses: see Clauses, Dependent

Reported Speech: see Indirect Speech

Subjects: The subject of a sentence is usually the performer, agent, or doer of the action of the verb. Be careful, however, as sometimes the subject can be an infinitive verb, a noun clause, or—in the case of passive voice sentences—the receiver of the action of the verb [see Passive Voice]. Also, a gerund noun (verb+ing) as a subject can be confusing.

EX: ***The moon*** *rose above the trees.*

            To understand punctuation *is an important skill.*

            That he had no regard for others *made him a menace to all he met.*

            Understanding punctuation *is an important skill.*

Syllables: Any good dictionary will show you where to break a word. This is helpful for pronunciation but, more, it is important for hyphen use in writing. When you come to the right margin of a page and a word is too long to fit, use a hyphen and break the word only between its syllables. Most word processing programs will do this automatically for you. Do not break a word if it leaves a single letter at the end of the top line or at the beginning of the next line.

Transitional Expressions: see Joining Words, Transitions

Verbs: see Parts of Speech

Editor's Note

Be aware that there are many very good style manuals available for a more in-depth investigation into punctuation use, writing guidelines, and language standards. Different fields often use different styles. How you write may need to conform to one of these certain styles. As there are slight differences among them, be sure to know which style you, your organization, association, editor, or educational institution follows:

The AMA Manual of Style: A Guide for Authors and Editors

The AP Stylebook (Associated Press)

APA Style (Publication Manual of the American Psychological Association)

The ASA Style Guide (American Sociological Association)

The Bluebook: A Uniform System of Citation (Harvard Law Review Association)

The Chicago Manual of Style (University of Chicago Press)

The MLA Handbook for Writers of Research Papers (Modern Language Association)

The MLA Style Manual and Guide to Scholarly Publishing (Modern Language Association)

The *New York Times* Manual of Style and Usage

Index

Ego uero exiftimabam pater errauiffe me
fic etiam nimis diu. B. P. Non eft
ita : fed ,ne nunc tandem erremus ; perge
de ignibus, ut propofuifti: uerum autem,
quid tu haeres? B. F: Per-
gam equidem , ut iubes: fed fcin , quam
in falebram inciderim ? B. P.
Nihil profecto minus. B. F.
Dum tibi ad ignes feftino , eam Aetnae
partem ; quae nobis una reftabat de tri-
bus (fic enim partiri foleo) ; et qua fine
ad ignes ipfos perueniri non poteft ; pe
nè omiferam fuboblitus : ita Aetnam ,
quafi Chimaeram , caecideramus ; et
tanquam ream , capite mulctaueramus
imprudentes : fed agam nunc tutius; ac
de utroq; fimul loquar. Superior itaq;
montis pars (nam iam de iis , quae in-
fra funt, diximus) ufq; ad fummum ca-
cumen nuda uariam faciem praeoften -
dit : nam alibi femiherbofi tractus funt
interfurgentibus tophis , qui etiam in

P. Bembo, *De Aetna*, an example of old punctuation.
(Venice, Aldus Manutius, 1494).